GETTING READY FOR CONTRACTS

A guide for voluntary organisations

GW00381370

GETTING READY FOR CONTRACTS

A guide for voluntary organisations

by
SANDY ADIRONDACK
and
RICHARD MACFARLANE

A Directory of Social Change publication

GETTING READY FOR CONTRACTS

By Sandy Adirondack and Richard Macfarlane
Cover design by Nicholas Karides
First published 1990
Published by the Directory of Social Change
© Directory of Social Change
Printed in Britain by Biddles of Guildford

ISBN 0-907164-64-1

Directory of Social Change, Radius Works, Back Lane, London NW3 1HL   Tel. 071-435 6524

Contents

Introduction

Although contractual arrangements between statutory authorities and the voluntary sector are not new, their use in the past has been fairly limited. With compulsory competitive tendering, community care and other government moves towards the contracting out of services, this will change. This represents a significant change in the role of voluntary organisations and how they are funded — a change which is of major importance to almost everyone in the voluntary sector. Only the smallest voluntary and community organisations, or those which are funded completely by donations, their own fundraising and charitable trusts, or those whose primary role is campaigning and advocacy are likely to be unaffected.

At the simplest level a contract is simply a new form of funding arrangement, more formal than a grant but in other ways not significantly different. But the 'contract culture' represents far more than a move towards formal and legally enforceable funding agreements.

The contract culture means a shift from relationships between a local authority or other statutory body as funder and the voluntary organisation as grant recipient, to relationships in which the statutory body is the **purchaser** of services and the voluntary organisation is the **provider** of those services. Using another form of new terminology, the voluntary organisation is a **contractor** and the statutory body becomes its **client**. (This can create considerable confusion about whether one is referring to the client as purchaser of services or user of services.)

Recognising that voluntary organisations needed information about contracts as well as opportunities to consider the organisational and management implications of the contract culture, the Directory of Social Change and the National Council for Voluntary Organisations jointly ran three five-day workshops in mid-1990. These were part of a pilot programme to develop workshops, courses and training materials to prepare voluntary organisations for contracts.

This book has been developed from the training materials which were produced for those workshops.

Chapter 1 looks, with a slightly sardonic tone, at various **organisational cultures** and how the people within these organisations will respond to the contract culture. Readers might find it interesting to try to position their own organisation.

Because no book can possibly cover everything that needs to be known about contracts and the contract culture, Chapter 2 provides a **booklist** on contracts in the voluntary sector, general management and financial management. We particularly recommend all the books on this list.

Chapter 3 is a checklist of **what to include in a contract**. No contract will exactly follow this format, but it will be a useful framework in thinking through what to include, or in knowing what to expect.

In Chapter 4 different **types of contracts** are explained, and some basic management points are raised.

Chapters 5 to 8 cover **legal issues** which must be considered when entering into contracts. Chapter 5 describes what a contract is in legal terms and what **contract law** covers. **Charities** may find that they cannot take on contracts to provide some activities and that they have to (or want to) set up a **separate trading organisation**; these issues are covered in Chapter 6.

Chapter 7 looks at the implications of **incorporation**, which can offer some protection to management committee members as the organisation takes on more complex legal responsibilities. Part of this chapter originally appeared in *Just About Managing? A guide to effective management for voluntary organisations and community groups* by Sandy Adirondack (London Voluntary Service Council, 1989) and another part will appear in *The Conduct of Local Government: A guide to the Local Government and Housing Act 1989* by Richard Gutch (National Council for Voluntary Organisations, 1990). We are grateful to LVSC and NCVO for permission to use these sections.

Grants are exempt from VAT; services provided under a contract generally are not, although some services provided by charities and other voluntary organisations may be exempt. Chapter 8 explains **VAT** and when registration is necessary.

Chapters 9 and 10 cover financial management issues. Parts of both first appeared in *Financial Planning and Control: A practical guide* by Richard Macfarlane (ICOM Co-Publications, 1986); ICOM Co-Publications kindly gave permission to reprint these sections. Chapter 9 explains the basics of **financial planning and control** for people who are not directly involved in finance. How to **cost** an activity and how to determine what **price** to charge are covered in Chapter 10.

Chapter 11 provides a basic introduction to **negotiation** and chapter 12 explains the **tendering** process.

How do you ensure that services provided under a contract continue to be relevant to users? Chapter 13 looks at issues around **quality of service, performance indicators, monitoring and evaluation.** Part of this chapter was originally published in *Just About Managing?*; again we are grateful to LVSC for permission to use it.

Last but not least, Chapter 14 consists of checklist of questions which organisations need to ask as part of the process of **getting ready for contracts.**

We hope you find this book useful, and that it helps you and your organisation prepare for contracts and the contract culture.

Sandy Adirondack
Richard Macfarlane
October 1990

1. How will you cope with contracts?

The move towards contracts may have little effect on your organisation, or it may profoundly change the nature of your work, the way you work, and even the people with whom your organisation works. The extent of change will depend on what you are now doing, whether it is what your funders want you to continue doing, and the type of funding arrangements you now have with your funders.

Regardless of the extent of change, individuals within any organisation will react in different ways. Their reactions will arise from their own personality, their perception of the organisation, their relationship to the organisation, their attitude towards the people who are advocating change, and the reasons for that change.

But organisations are more than the sum of the individuals involved. They have a culture of their own, determined by their users, their workers and their committee members, but also determined by many other factors including:

- the organisation's history;
- its philosophy, ethos or general approach to its work;
- the role of users or members within the organisation;
- its relationships with other agencies (voluntary, public, commercial);
- whether it is a branch of a larger organisation;
- its size;
- its sources of funding.

An organisation's approach to the opportunities and pitfalls presented by contracts will be affected by its culture. Problems may arise if the organisation is forced into actions which run contrary to its basic culture.

Some organisational cultures, possible attitudes towards the changes signalled by the move towards contracts, and the risks attached to such attitudes are outlined here (perhaps slightly tongue-in-cheek).

Eager for change

Trendy

The trendy organisation takes on the latest fashion, without thinking about whether it is good or bad for the organisation or its users. Its key word is 'flavour of the month'. It is likely to rush into contracts not because this is best for the users, but in order to be the first to do it. The trendy organisation will probably give inadequate attention to effects on users or staff, or practical changes required in the organisation.

Innovative

An organisation which wants to be considered innovative constantly sets up or takes on new activities, often before existing activities have been put on a solid footing. With 'pilot project' as its key word, it is likely to bid for new activities or to leap at the chance to take on local authority services. It may ignore existing activities, and will very likely ignore settled work routines. The risk is that it could end up unhappily committed to long-term provision of an activity which ceases to be exciting.

Expansionist

For expansionists, the key word is 'growth'. The organisation may not be particularly trendy or innovative, but wants to expand existing services at a rapid rate. It is likely to take on activities similar to what it is already doing, but with much larger numbers. It could find itself unable to cope with the increased management and financial responsibilities which follow rapid expansion.

Entrepreneurial

An entrepreneurial organisation welcomes the chance to move into the world of business and to compete with other agencies and sectors, seeing its key word as 'risk-taking'. An entrepreneurial approach is often, but not always, linked with expansionism. This type of organisation could end up losing its identity as a voluntary organisation, becoming virtually indistinguishable from commercial sector businesses.

Professional

There is a difference between professionalism (to be welcomed) and professionalisation. An organisation which defines itself primarily as professional is probably talking about the latter, and is more keen to develop the professional expertise of its workers than to develop professional-quality services for users. Contracts are welcomed because they provide an ideal opportunity for staff to learn about law, finance and high-level negotiation. In the professionalised organisation the key words will be 'training' and 'career structure'. Such an organisation may not pay much attention to the needs of users, especially if users are resistant to change.

Giving in to change

Sell-out

While protesting loudly about the privatisation of the welfare state, this organisation quickly commits itself to taking on contracted-out services without seriously considering whether there are alternatives for the organisation. Its key phrase is 'TINA' — there is no alternative. This type of organisation could end up with endless internal arguments and splits.

Reluctant

The reluctant organisation feels it has no choice but to go along with whatever the local authority, health authority or other funder is suggesting, even though it doesn't really want to. Its key word is 'pragmatism'. Pressured by external forces, it may lose sight of its own reason for existence, its own 'mission' and objectives.

Resisting change

Ostrich

With its head in the sand, this organisation does not think that its type of work, or its funding agency, or its size of organisation will be affected by contracts. Although its key word is 'stability', it could end up having to make complex decisions at the last minute without adequate preparation or consultation.

Participative

Still fully committed to the participative ethos of its early days, this organisation involves all users, staff, volunteers and committee members in lengthy discussions about the implications of contracts and insists on reaching unanimous 'consensus' before deciding to take them on. Its key word is 'consultation', which is a good thing — but it could end up spending so much time on the process of deciding what to do that there is not enough time to plan how to do it.

Over-cautious

The overly cautious organisation comes up with all the reasons why it should not change, expand, take on new commitments or activities, or change the way it does things now. The key phrase is 'avoid unnecessary risk'. It will not end up over-committed, but it may become stagnant, lose creative workers and members, and even lose its funding because of its refusal to adapt to new circumstances.

Right-on

Although similar to the *Sell-Out* in its basic beliefs, the right-on organisation commits itself to *not* taking on contracts, without seriously considering the implications. Its key phrase is 'ideological purity'. It could end up broke and/or non-existent, after endless internal arguments and splits.

Sensible about change

The sensible, reasonable organisation is probably yours. Your organisational culture is one which allows the necessary time for people to learn everything possible about a potential change, consider the implications, consult with others who will be affected, and make a clear decision on the basis of what is best for the organisation's users, the community at large, staff and volunteers, and the organisation as an ongoing entity.

The trendies, innovators, expansionists, entrepreneurs and professionals are eager to embrace the contract culture. This has positive aspects, but too rapid change or growth may have long-term negative effects.

The sell-outs and the reluctant pragmatists give in to external pressures without fully considering the effects on the organisation.

The ostriches, participatives, over-cautious and right-ons may find themselves left behind as the voluntary sector moves towards new funding arrangements and takes on new services and activities.

Sensible organisations are those which are taking action now to ensure that they can take advantage of the contract culture, without jeopardising their current activities or losing sight of their objectives. This book is part of the process of getting relevant information, weighing up the advantages and disadvantages of contracts, and ensuring that the major considerations in any new arrangements are the service and its users.

Which type of organisation are you?

2. Essential reading

In some local authority and health authority areas and in some types of work contracts are being introduced very quickly; in other areas and sectors very little has been done. There are different types of contracts, different pressures, different issues. It is impossible for any one course, seminar or publication to cover everything; and even if it could cover everything much of the information would probably be out of date within a few months.

It is therefore essential to keep up to date with the latest information and publications relevant to your type of work and your funders. New materials are constantly being published on the issues raised by contracting in the voluntary sector. To keep abreast of what is happening:

- Subscribe to *NCVO News* (National Council for Voluntary Organisations, 26 Bedford Square, London WC1B 3HU, tel 071-636 4066). This monthly bulletin reports on all significant changes in the voluntary sector and indicates where to get more information on each topic.

- Subscribe to the quarterly bulletin *Contracting - In or Out?* produced by NCVO in conjunction with the Voluntary Sector Working Group on Contracting. Free from the Local Voluntary Action Department at NCVO, it covers current issues and changes in contracting and summarises what is happening in various local authority areas.

- Get on the mailing list for the Directory of Social Change's 'Charity Bookstore' (Radius Works, Back Lane, London NW3 1HL, tel 071-435 8171). DoSC will distribute all major publications about contracting in the voluntary sector, as well as many other important books and reports.

- Your local Council for Voluntary Service should be well aware of what is happening in your area, not only about contracts but about all funding arrangements and voluntary/statutory sector partnerships.

- If there is a national, regional or local network or umbrella organisation for your type of work, it should be able to provide helpful information.

Publications on contracting

This book does not seek to cover all the issues around contracting, so you will need to read other publications as well. This booklist, which is current to September 1990, includes only items which are particularly recommended. Large organisations may want to buy most of them; smaller organisations may be able to borrow them from their local council for voluntary service or from a network or umbrella organisation for their type of work.

Contracts for Social Care: The local authority view
(Association of Metropolitan Authorities, 1990. A4, 50pp. ISBN 0-902052-85-3. £10 from AMA, 35 Great Smith St, London SW1P 3BJ, or Directory of Social Change.) Although it seems expensive, look on it as costing only 20p per page — and each page is worth it. This thoughtful pamphlet considers the changing relationship between local authorities (as purchasers of care services) and voluntary organisations (as providers of the services). Special emphasis is given to the importance of user involvement in contract specification, and to monitoring performance. Although written from the local authority perspective it is essential reading for voluntary organisations. There are detailed recommendations for good practice, and lots of useful checklists. It is oriented towards organisations providing care services but most of it is relevant to other voluntary organisations as well.

Contracting - In or Out? Guidance notes on contracting for voluntary groups
Published by NCVO, these guidance notes are £3 each from NCVO's Local Voluntary Action Department or Directory of Social Change (addresses above).
No.1. The legal context, by Nick Fielding and Richard Gutch. (September 1989. A4, 17pp.)
Easy-to-read introduction to the issues including compulsory competitive tendering, implications for charities, pros and cons of incorporation, and the Local Government Act 1989. Although slightly out of date, it is still a good basic introduction.
No.2. The contract culture: The challenge for voluntary organisations (November 1989. A4, 28pp.)
Sets the context for contracting and provides a clear outline of problems and opportunities presented by contracting, and a list of issues which voluntary organisations must address.
No.3. The impact on management and organisation, by Richard Macfarlane. (April 1990. A4, 20pp.)
Focuses on the management issues which arise for voluntary organisations entering into contractual arrangements, specifically the changes required in the processes of decision-making.
Further guidance notes will be published.

Twelve Charity Contracts
By Anne Davies and Ken Edwards. (Directory of Social Change, 1990. A5, 128pp. ISBN 0-907164-59-5. £7.95 from Directory of Social Change.)
Based on interviews with people involved in 12 voluntary organisations which have entered into various types of contracts, this book gives a fascinating insight into some of the problems they faced and the opportunities they perceive. Also includes sample contracts for most of the organisations. But be warned: don't use the contracts as models without thinking through the implications for your own organisation.

Service Contracts: Guidelines for a local code of practice
(London Voluntary Service Council, 1990. A4, 6pp. £1.50 from LVSC, 68 Chalton St, London NW1 1JR.)
Intended to help local authorities incorporate the interests of voluntary organisations into an overall framework for community

care plans and other new arrangements for service provision and funding.

Contracts for Care

The Community Care Project at NCVO publishes a number of information sheets, briefing papers, conference reports and a newsletter on contracts for community care. Most of the issues are relevant to contracts for other types of services. Full details of all current publications are available from the Community Care Project at NCVO.

Bidding for Change? Voluntary organisations and competitive tendering for local authority services

By Christian Kunz, Rowan Jones and Ken Spencer. (Birmingham Settlement and Community Projects Foundation, 1989. A4, 40pp. ISBN 0-907272-11-8. £3 from Birmingham Settlement, 318 Sumner Lane, Birmingham B19 3RL or Community Development Foundation, 60 Highbury Grove, London N5 2AG.)

Looks at the issues around compulsory competitive tendering (CCT) and non-compulsory or voluntary competitive tendering: advantages and disadvantages of bidding for contracts, how you go about bidding, and how to develop these new forms of partnership with statutory authorities.

Publications on management

Any booklist on management is necessarily a partial selection. Nonetheless we particularly recommend these. All are available from the Directory of Social Change, Radius Works, Back Lane, London NW3 1HL (tel 071-435 8171) unless indicated otherwise.

In addition to these, Kogan Page publishes a wide range of inexpensive books on management and finance in small businesses. They are not oriented towards the voluntary sector but many are clearly applicable. Kogan Page also has books on specific types of business, such as catering or transport, which can be very useful. A publications list is available from Kogan Page, 120 Pentonville Road, London N1 9JN (tel 071-278 0433).

General management and planning

Just About Managing? A guide to effective management for voluntary organisations and community groups
By Sandy Adirondack. (London Voluntary Service Council, 1989. A4, 109pp. ISBN 0-901171-85-9. £7.50 from LVSC, 68 Chalton St, London NW1 1JR or Directory of Social Change.)
A practical guide providing a basic but comprehensive introduction to good management, including decision-making, planning, monitoring, evaluation and finance, as well as time and stress management.

Planning Together: The art of effective teamwork
By George Gawlinski and Lois Graessle. (Bedford Square Press, 1988. A4, 88pp. ISBN 0-7199-1202-4. £9.95 from Directory of Social Change.)
A lovely book, well illustrated with many useful procedures and exercises to help groups set objectives, organise themselves and work better together.

Croner's Management of Voluntary Organisations
(Croner Publications, 1989 + quarterly updates. Lots of pages. £39.70 from Directory of Social Change.)
Croner's is well known for its looseleaf binders on many aspects of management, employment, etc. This one, especially for the voluntary sector, contains a great deal of legal and practical information, but is expensive and difficult to find your way around.

Legal structures and charitable status

Voluntary But Not Amateur: A guide to the law for voluntary organisations and community groups
By Duncan Forbes, Ruth Hayes and Jacki Reason. (London Voluntary Service Council, 3rd ed, 1990. A4, 101pp. ISBN 0-901171-95-6. £7.95 from LVSC, 68 Chalton St, London NW1 1JR or Directory of Social Change.)
Third edition of the ever-popular legal guide which includes a very straightforward introduction to advantages and

disadvantages of various legal structures, as well as to all legal issues affecting voluntary organisations.

Charitable Status: A practical handbook

By Andrew Phillips. (InterChange Books, 3rd ed, 1988. A5, 105pp. ISBN 0-948309-05-9. £5.95 from Directory of Social Change.)
Essential introductory guide for any organisation which has, or is considering applying for, charitable status.

A Guide to the Benefits of Charitable Status

By Michael Norton. (Directory of Social Change, 2nd ed, 1988. A5, 230pp. ISBN 0-907164-26-9. £5.95 from Directory of Social Change.)
Provides a more detailed explanation of the legal issues affecting charities.

A Practical Guide to Company Law for Voluntary Organisations

By Bev Cross. (Currently out of print but is being revised and will be available in 1991, £5.95 from Directory of Social Change.)
Any organisation which is incorporated or is weighing up whether to incorporate should have this comprehensive and well-structured summary of company law relevant to voluntary organisations. Includes advantages and disadvantages of becoming a company, charitable company or industrial and provident society, how to set up a company, and responsibilities of company directors and the company secretary.

Legal Structures for Voluntary Organisations and Community Groups: A guide to the available literature

(Legal Structures Group, 1989. A5, 46pp. ISBN 0-9514541-0-2. £2.95 from Legal Structures Group c/o BMCVS, 19-25 Sunbridge Road, Bradford BD1 2AY.)
Primarily an annotated bibliography, but also summarises the types of legal structure and contains a good section on where to find specimen governing instruments (constitutions) for various types of organisation, including community businesses and co-operatives.

Financial planning and management

Accounting and Financial Management for Charities
By Michael Norton and Hilary Blume. (Directory of Social Change, 1985. A4, 106pp. ISBN 0-907164-18-8. £7.95 from Directory of Social Change.)
A clear, readable guide on how to keep accounts and financial management, plus sample exercises.

Financial Planning and Control: A practical guide
By Richard Macfarlane. (ICOM Co-Publications, 1986. A5, 128pp. ISBN 0-946776-08-3. £5.30 from Turnaround Distribution, 27 Horsell Road, London N5.
Intended for workers cooperatives, but the principles and practice of preparing a business plan are the same whether you're a co-op, a community business or a voluntary organisation involved in contracts. More oriented towards 'business' than the DoSC book above, which is primarily about grants and fundraising.

Negotiation

Successful Negotiation
By Robert B Maddux. (Kogan Page, 1988. A5, 62pp. ISBN 1-85091-741-8. £3.99 from bookshops or Kogan Page, 120 Pentonville Road, London N1 9JN.)
The basics of negotiation skills, in a straightforward little book which can be read in less than an hour.

Getting to Yes: Negotiating agreement without giving in
By Roger Fisher and William Ury. (Hutchinson Business Books, 1981. A5, 162pp. ISBN 0-09-164071-7. £5.95 from bookshops or Directory of Social Change.)
Classic book on 'principled' or 'win/win' negotiation. Essential reading not just for contracts but for all the other negotiations you are involved in.

3. What to include in a contract

This chapter cannot cover everything an individual organisation or statutory authority might want to include in a contract, nor will all contracts need to cover all the terms outlined here. However it can be used as a starting point.

Contracts do not have to be written in complex legal language, although the legal department of a local authority or health authority or your own lawyer might insist that they are. When you are considering a contract (or, indeed, any other form of funding agreement) it would be sensible to go through this checklist and write down, in your own language, what you think the contract should include. This document then serves as a starting point for negotiations, and as a reference point to ensure that your organisation does not get coerced into accepting conditions which it does not want.

In this checklist 'purchaser' refers to the local authority, health authority or other agency which is buying and paying for a service. 'Contractor' refers to the voluntary organisation which is selling and providing the service.

1. Introduction

    a. Who the parties are to the contract.

       If the voluntary organisation is not incorporated (i.e. if it is not a company or an industrial and provident society) it cannot legally enter into a contract in its own name. Frequently this point is overlooked and the organisation is given as one of the parties. If the point is not overlooked, the contract may be with one or two people (usually the management committee chair and secretary or chair and treasurer); the contract *must* indicate that they are entering into the contract on behalf of the organisation.

b. The statutory powers under which the local authority, health authority or other statutory body is acting.

c. The powers under which the voluntary organisation is acting. If this is included, it will be by reference to the objects clause in the organisation's constitution. (If you are not sure whether your objects cover the work you are taking on, or whether your organisation has the power to enter into a contract, check with a solicitor or, if the organisation is a charity, with the Charity Commission.)

d. The date the contract comes into force, and its duration (how long it lasts, and/or when it ends).

e. The position or post-holder within the purchaser agency with responsibility for administering the contract (authorised officer).

f. The position or post-holder within the contractor with responsibility for administering the contract (the contract manager).

2. Services, activities or facilities to be provided

a. The types of services, activities or facilities to be provided and what the objectives are. This can be as vague or as explicit as the parties want. Often it is better to give a fairly broad overview in the body of the contract, and to refer to an appendix or schedule which gives more detail about the services. (Note that 'services' in this chapter means services, activities, facilities or whatever the voluntary organisation is providing.)

b. Where the services will be located or provided.

c. When the services are to be provided. Whether services are cyclical or whether there are timetables or deadlines to be met.

d. Who the services are for, and criteria by which users will be selected or referred for them. This might include, for example, equal opportunities considerations, nomination rights by the purchaser, degree of disability or frailty, age limits, catchment area or geographic areas covered or other limits on who is served.

e. Limits, if any, on numbers of users.

f. A statement that all decisions about eligibility for services and method of provision, other than those specifically covered by the contract, are to be made by the contractor.

g. Indication of how users or others are to be involved in decisions about the services.

h. Standards of service to be provided, and criteria by which services will be assessed (sometimes called performance indicators, service objectives, etc). These standards might be related to jointly agreed codes of practice or guidelines, which should be referred to in the contract and/or be included as appendices.

i. Whether fees can be charged for services, and if so how these are to be determined.

j. Procedures for dealing with complaints by users.

k. How the services relate to the overall plan for users in the local authority or health authority area, relationship to services provided by other agencies, etc.

l. Support (if any) to be provided by the purchaser, for example access to vehicle maintenance, local authority training courses or architects. The terms on which such support is to be provided.

m. Possibility of sub-contracting, and the contractor's responsibility for overseeing sub-contracted work.

n. Copyright for written, audio-visual or other materials produced by or about the services.

3. Equality of opportunity

a. Compliance with equal opportunities policies and legislation.

b. Provision for ensuring fair access to services and for ensuring that no one is denied access to services or receives a poorer service because of race, ethnic origin, religious belief, disability, gender, age, marital status, being a gay man or lesbian (except insofar as services are limited to people of particular groups).

c. Requirements for translation, interpretation, special facilities etc.

4. Management decisions

a. What decisions about the running of the services the purchaser will expect to be consulted on, for example

referrals, and what will be the sole responsibility of the contractor.
b. Procedures for such consultation, and for resolving disputes.
c. Involvement of the purchaser's representative(s) in the contractor's management committee or other body, and a statement that such representative(s) shall not have voting rights on any matter relating to the contract.
d. Confidentiality of information obtained by the purchaser or contractor under the contract (especially information about individuals).

5. Monitoring and evaluation

a. Arrangements, if required, for a liaison group or similar group to oversee or advise on services provided under the contract. How members are selected, who they are accountable to, what powers the group has. How users are represented on such a group.
b. Monitoring reports to the purchaser or the liaison group. Frequency of such reports. What reports need to cover, including provision for feedback from users. How services will be assessed, and by whom.
c. Other monitoring procedures, for example periodic inspections, surveys of users, meetings with users, independent (external) assessment.
d. Under what circumstances the purchaser has access to premises or services run by the contractor under the contract.
e. Provision for annual or other formal evaluation reviews.
f. Procedures for negotiating changes in services due to changing needs or demand.

6. Premises or accommodation

a. Terms and conditions under which the contractor occupies or uses any premises provided by the purchaser.
b. Responsibilities for insuring premises.
c. Responsibility for maintenance and repair of premises.
d. Support from the purchaser, for example access to local authority architects.

e.   Health and safety requirements.

7. Equipment and vehicles

a.   Terms and conditions under which the contractor uses any equipment or vehicles provided by the purchaser.
b.   Responsibility for insuring contents, special equipment, vehicles, drivers.
c.   Responsibility for maintenance, cleaning, repair and replacement.
d.   Ownership of existing and replacement equipment, vehicles, etc. (If the contractor subsequently loses the contract, who owns the equipment?)
e.   Support from the purchaser, for example access to vehicle servicing.

8. Costs and payment

a.   Basis for pricing, e.g. per capita payments, fixed fee payments, cost-plus payment.
b.   The cost of the services in the first year. The total cost may be included in the contract with a detailed budget attached as an appendix or schedule. When working this out, ensure that all costs are included, for example locum or holiday cover, pensions, allowance for maternity or sickness cover, VAT, allowance for inflation.
c.   Management costs, costs involved in preparatory work for the contract, setting-up costs.
d.   Provision, if any, for increases during the year (for example if new salary scales are negotiated, or if per capita costs increase unexpectedly).
e.   How the purchaser will pay (quarterly, half-yearly, annually), when the services will be paid for (in advance, midway through the period, in arrears), and deadlines for payments.
f.   Whether payment is contingent on the purchaser receiving financial reports.
g.   What happens with the underspend if the contractor can make savings in the provision of the services, or if funds are received from other sources.

9. Financial monitoring and review

a. Financial reports to be provided by the contractor to the purchaser: how often, how much information, how they will be monitored.

b. When annual accounts have to be provided to the purchaser.

c. When budgets for the next year have to be submitted to the purchaser.

d. Procedures and timetables for negotiating agreed budgets for future years.

e. Procedures for reviewing unforeseen financial costs.

10. Staffing and volunteers

a. Any provisions relating to terms and conditions of employment.

b. Any requirements for staff qualifications and/or experience, including 'genuine occupational qualifications' as defined under the Race Relations Act 1976 and Sex Discrimination Act 1975.

c. Detailed provision if the contractor is taking over staff from the statutory authority or other employer, including employees' right to continuous employment, trade union arrangements, what happens to transferred employees if the contractor subsequently loses the contract, etc.

d. Involvement by purchaser in staff recruitment and selection.

e. Circumstances, if any, in which the contractor should submit details of staff to enable the local authority to undertake necessary police checks.

f. Use of part-time and/or agency staff.

g. Whether volunteers are to be involved in providing the service.

h. Training or other support to be provided to employees or volunteers.

11. Indemnity and insurance

a. Responsibility for public liability insurance and any insurance specific to the provision of the services.

b. Responsibility for underwriting damages not covered by insurances.

12. Enforcement and disputes

a. Procedures for review and negotiation if the contractor finds itself unable to fulfil any part of the agreement. This should include timescales within which decisions need to be made, the process for renegotiation, who is authorised to renegotiate, opportunity for the purchaser to purchase other services, and procedures for termination.

b. Procedures in case of complaints by the purchaser about the contractor or the services provided.

c. Procedures for resolving disputes between the parties, including procedures for third party arbitration if the parties to the contract cannot agree.

d. Procedures in case of inadequate performance or non-performance by the contractor (breach of contract).

e. Procedures in case of non-payment or other breach by purchaser. What happens if payments are not received by the deadline (e.g. a penalty clause, or clause saying the purchaser becomes liable for any bank charges and interest if the contractor has to borrow money because of the delay).

f. Procedures in case of termination of the agreement because of breach, including period of notice required, and what happens to money paid to the contractor but not yet spent.

13. Review, variation and extension

a. Procedures for altering or varying the contract.

b. Procedures and timetable for renegotiating an extension to the contract before it expires. (Try for a rolling contract, in which one year is added on to the contract at each annual review. So a three-year contract, for example, is always for three years, rather than being for three years then two years then one year then three years again.)

c. Procedures and timetable for termination not involving breach, either during the contract or when it expires.

14. Notice

a. There is sometimes a clause specifying where reports, notices etc have to be delivered.

15. Signatures and dates

Note that anyone signing on behalf of an organisation *must* be authorised to do so, and must specify that they are signing *on behalf of the organisation*.
Otherwise they could be held individually responsible.

Most contracts go through several drafts before they are finally signed. Be sure that each draft is:

- dated on the top of page 1, so it is easy to see which is the most recent version;
- clearly marked 'draft' on *every* page.

No matter how many drafts you have read through, always look carefully at the most recent version. An apparently minor change in wording or a typing mistake may have significant implications. If you do not understand something, or have misgivings about what it might mean, ask for an explanation in writing.

This is especially important if the contract is written in legal language which appears incomprehensible. **Any legal concept can be expressed in terms which a non-specialist can understand. You are signing the contract; you have a right (indeed, an obligation) to understand what you are signing.**

Chapters 11 and 12 (negotiating a contract and tendering for a contract) explain the stages in negotiating and drawing up a contract.

4. Contracts in the voluntary sector

Contracts between voluntary organisations and the agencies paying for services, activities or facilities can be broadly divided into two types: those which you do not have to compete for (contracts issued non-competitively) and those which you do have to compete for (competitive tendering).

Competitive tendering is further divided into two types: situations in which a local authority must by law ask for competitive bids (compulsory competitive tendering or CCT) and situations in which the local authority or other agency voluntarily decides to ask for competitive bids (non-compulsory or voluntary competitive tendering).

This chapter briefly describes the differences between the types of contract, and looks at some of the initial steps in preparing for contracts. The term 'service' means any services, activities or facilities provided by a voluntary organisation.

Contracts issued non-competitively

A contract which is issued without competition is often not significantly different from a fairly formal grant agreement. The purchaser (local authority, health authority etc) and the contractor (voluntary organisation) agree the services to be provided and negotiate the terms. These are formalised in a written agreement which might (or might not) be called a contract.

Grant-aid contracts and funding contracts

The typical grant-aid procedure is for a voluntary organisation to define the services, activities or facilities it wants to provide, and to apply to a statutory authority or other body for funding. If the funding is provided, it will usually be called a grant. The grant might or might not be accompanied by detailed conditions.

Increasingly the grant conditions are being formalised. Some funders are calling these more formal agreements grant-aid contracts or funding contracts. Even though it is called a contract, it is issued through the grant application procedure, and in legal terms there is confusion about whether it is a grant or a contract for services.

One of the main reasons for this formalisation is to put a greater emphasis on *outcomes* or *outputs*: what the voluntary organisation and the local authority or other funder expect to be achieved as a result of the expenditure. The funder will then use these outputs to justify its expenditure in terms of cost effectiveness. This is very different from the traditional approach in which the local authority or other funder, having made a grant, is concerned primarily about whether the money is spent for the purposes specified in the grant application.

The distinction between a grant and a contract is significant for corporation tax (see Chapter 7), for VAT (Chapter 8) and for some other purposes. It is also significant in terms of enforcement; something which is not a contract cannot be enforced in the same way as something which is a contract.

The National Council for Voluntary Organisations is seeking legal advice on the extent to which 'grants' are legally enforceable as contracts.

Service agreements and service contracts

A service contract or service agreement is an agreement between the purchaser and contractor under which the contractor provides services, activities or facilities and is paid to do so by the purchaser. This is different from a grant because the purchaser is *paying the contractor to provide a service*; it is a straightforward business deal. It does not matter whether the service to be provided is defined in a general way or in great detail, or whether the piece of paper is called an agreement or a contract.

One differentiating factor in different types of agreement is who defines what is to be provided. In the typical grant application process, the voluntary organisation examines the local authority's or other funder's policies and provision, identifies gaps in provision and defines what it wants to provide. For a service contract or service agreement, the service to be provided might be defined by the voluntary organisation (contractor) or by the statutory authority (purchaser), or might be negotiated between them.

With the growth of community care, local authorities will define the services which need to be provided, and will purchase those services. Although they might invite competitive bids to provide the services they are under no obligation to do so, and in many cases they will issue contracts for services without competition. The same process is happening in many other sectors not directly related to community care. This non-competitive process will give rise to what we are calling service contracts.

The Association of Metropolitan Authorities distinguishes between a **performance contract** which defines what is to be provided or achieved, and a **method contract** which defines how a particular aim is to be achieved.

The move towards service contracts is occurring within a framework of rapidly changing relationships between statutory authorities and the voluntary sector. The borderline between grant and contract is blurred at the moment, but what is clear is that over the next few years most statutory authorities will be moving towards more formal and legally enforceable relationships with the voluntary sector.

Competitive tendering

Under competitive tendering, the statutory authority issues a tender specification describing a particular service or activity and invites tenders (bids) from organisations which want to provide the service. It then chooses which one will get the contract to do so. This process is described in more detail in chapter 12.

A voluntary organisation which wants to ensure that a service is relevant to its users may be able to influence the tender specification for that service. But it may be open to charges of conflict of interest if it later tenders for the contract. This is a delicate area, and in some cases it can be useful for one part of an organisation to be involved in campaigning or advocacy work (ensuring that services are relevant) while another part is involved in tendering and providing services under contract.

Under the Local Government Act 1988 local authorities must put certain defined services out to competitive tender; this is referred to as compulsory competitive tendering (CCT). An authority may choose to put other services out to tender; this is voluntary or non-compulsory competitive tendering.

The tender specification might define the service in great detail, including what is to be provided, where, when and for whom. The contract will then be granted to the bidder who can best provide this service; in reality this often means the bidder who can provide it most cheaply. In other cases the tender specification might describe the service only in the most general terms, and invite bids in which each bidder defines how it would provide the service. In this case there is much more scope for the bidder to define what is provided.

An organisation considering whether to tender for a contract must ask itself some searching questions:

- Do we have the knowledge and the time to prepare a tender bid? If we do not have them, can we afford to buy them in?
- Can we justify putting time, money and energy into preparing a bid for a contract we might not get?
- Can we be realistic about what it will cost us to provide the services required under this contract, or will we be tempted to bid too low?

Getting involved in competitive tendering has many implications for voluntary organisations. They are likely to be competing against other local organisations involved in similar work; this is unpleasant, and also gives rise to complex conflicts of interest if someone from one organisation is, say, on the management committee of another organisation and both groups are competing for the same contract. They may also be competing against commercial organisations which may not be prepared to provide the same good terms and conditions for employees and quality of service which the voluntary organisation is proposing, which may give them a competitive edge (in financial terms).

Competitive tendering is likely to prove difficult for small or new organisations which do not have access to complex managerial, financial and legal skills. Larger or better established organisations have a moral obligation to develop joint bids with smaller organisations or to consider sub-contracting work to those groups.

Getting organised for contracts

For some organisations the shift from a grant-aid culture to the contract culture may be no more than a change in terminology. For others it will mean significant, and perhaps very painful, decisions. The contract culture will mean many new opportunities for the voluntary sector: new types of partnership with the public sector and perhaps with the commercial sector, new ways of working, new services or activities to be provided. But it will also mean many new pressures. If voluntary organisations are not to collapse under the weight of change, they must plan carefully.

The delay in implementation of the government's community care proposals highlights the pressures on all bodies — whether statutory, voluntary or commercial — involved in these new partnerships. In mid-1990 there was a sense of panic (how would everything be in place by April 1991?), and anticipation (how would this new approach affect the users and providers of care services?). The postponement was met with relief by organisations not yet prepared for the changes, and with dismay by those which had already geared themselves up.

The delay provided the opportunity for very careful preparation, which can only be of benefit to organisations which seriously want to enter the contract culture. But the delay also illustrates the extent to which organisations involved in the contract culture are at the mercy of unpredictable political decisions.

Clarifying core objectives

What would the response be if you individually asked each person involved in your organisation — all the users, the volunteers, the management committee members and the staff — 'Do you know what the core purpose of this organisation is?'. Some of them might say no, or give a waffly answer. But probably most would say yes, and would proceed to tell you with great certainty and clarity what the core purpose is. The only problem is that at the end of this exercise, you would probably have as many variants on 'core purpose' as you have respondents.

Everyone involved with an organisation will perceive it differently, know different things about its origins and history, have a different understanding of its philosophy and approach, and want different things from it. An important factor in preparing for contracts, indeed an important factor in good management generally, is bringing these different perceptions together into a coherent and shared view of what the organisation is and what it should be doing.

This means creating opportunities for people to learn about the organisation, re-affirm its core purpose or 'mission', set clear objectives for the next few years, discuss its current work and future possibilities, and set priorities for the immediate future. Without such opportunities any organisation is in danger of losing its sense of direction, or going in too many directions at once, or responding opportunistically to every new idea or demand for change.

So a first step in preparing for the contract culture is to ensure that the organisation has a clear sense of its own identity, its objects and overall purpose and its current objectives and priorities, and to ensure that there are regular procedures to allow these to be shared and discussed. If the core purpose, objectives and priorities are all clear, it becomes much easier to decide whether a new funding arrangement or a new activity is appropriate—or whether it is an organisational tail being wagged by the funding dog.

Avoiding panic decisions

There is a tendency for public authorities to take a long time to organise themselves for a tender or a contract, and then to demand that voluntary organisations (who often have a strong commitment to participative decision-making) respond with a speed that makes good decision-making impossible. You can deal with this in two ways.

- Anticipate, well in advance, which activities the local authority might ask you to take on under contract, or might put out to tender. Think about exactly what they might specify, and whether and under what conditions your organisation could take on the activities. Set up a **contracts working group** or **contracts sub-committee** made up of staff, management committee members and users to start thinking about the opportunities and potential pitfalls. Don't be caught unawares by something you could have anticipated.

- In your dealings with the local authority or other body, try to ensure that they understand the importance of allowing adequate time for discussion and decision-making within voluntary organisations. If an activity is being put out to tender, encourage the local authority or other body to issue a realistic timetable as part of the specification.

Delegation

At an early stage in planning for contracts the organisation should decide how it is going to deal with the work and the decision-making that will be necessary for these new arrangements. Of particular importance will be a clear delegation of authority to staff, management committee members and/or charity trustees to discuss the details of the proposal, agree any written tender bid, and agree the final contract details.

The limits of this delegated authority, together with a process for review and formal approval, should be explicitly discussed and decided and should be recorded in a minute of the management committee or other appropriate body. It may be helpful to keep in mind the difference between **informing** people about what is happening, **discussing** ideas, **consulting** people (getting their ideas and opinions, **making a proposal** or proposals about possible courses of action, **recommending** a particular course of action, and **deciding** what should be done.

If, for example, a contracts working group or contracts sub-committee is set up or if responsibility is delegated to the organisation's policy and development sub-committee, everyone should be clear about whether the sub-group is expected to bring draft proposals for a tender bid back to the main group (probably the management committee), or whether the group can proceed with the bid without any further formal approval from the main group.

Similarly, can a person or the people negotiating on behalf of the organisation change anything, or does everything have to come back to the sub-group and/or main group for approval?

If an individual or sub-group with delegated authority oversteps the mark, avoid the temptation to criticise and blame. Clarify what should happen in a similar situation next time, then move on.

Bear in mind that there will be conflicts of interest for anyone involved in your organisation who is directly linked to the purchaser (local authority etc), or who is involved with another organisation which might be tendering for the same contract. When contracts are discussed opportunity must be given for people to declare any conflict of interest and, depending on the circumstances, they should be excluded from the discussion as a whole or from any decision or vote on the issue.

Resources for the contract culture

The process of tendering for a contract or negotiating a contract will, if done properly, require a substantial input of resources from the voluntary organisation. This will be of four types:

- staff time and attention;
- management committee and/or trustee time and attention;
- specialist legal, financial and other advice that may have to be paid for;
- administrative services for producing and circulating documents.

You must plan for these demands on your time and money; this may mean cutting back on existing activities, or seeking additional funding to cover the extra costs.

In addition, contracts will require detailed financial and service monitoring, regular review and evaluation of provision against specification, renegotiation of specifications, and in due course negotiations for renewal of the contract. This implies a continuing commitment of staff, committee, specialist and administrative time and attention. The financial, management and service implications of this commitment must be kept in mind.

5. Legal aspects of contracts

It is not necessary to be an expert on contract law to enter successfully into contractual agreements, since you will probably want to take legal advice. But it can be helpful at least to understand some of the basic legal concepts.

This chapter provides a very brief overview of the points in contract law which might be relevant to voluntary organisations considering providing services under contracts with local authorities, health authorities etc. It does not cover consumer contracts or employment contracts, although most of the same principles apply.

The information in this chapter is based on *Contract Law in Perspective* by John Tillotson (Butterworths, 2nd ed, 1985, ISBN 0-406-66621-0, £8.95 from bookshops) and all the quotations are from this source. If you are particularly interested in the legal aspects of contracts, most good bookshops and libraries will have A-level or college textbooks on contract law.

Theoretical background

Legal and business views of contract

In business terms, a contract is a way to ensure that goods or services are efficiently produced, sold and delivered. In legal terms, however, the focus is on the rights and obligations of each party, and what happens if a contract breaks down. The idea of 'contract' includes both these perspectives: efficiency, and rights and obligations.

A contract always involves an exchange. From the **business perspective** a contract involves 'rational planning of the transaction with careful provision for as many future contingencies as can be foreseen'; from the **legal perspective** a contract involves 'the existence or use of actual or potential legal sanctions to induce performance of the exchange or to compensate for non-performance'.

Contract law covers not only rights, obligations and the quest for efficiency, but also seeks to balance the often conflicting aims of certainty (a legal framework in which planned relationships can proceed with confidence) and flexibility (to allow for the reality of a constantly changing business environment).

Contract law

The purpose of contract law is to prevent disputes from arising or from getting to the stage of litigation (legal action). It does this by encouraging the parties to the contract to plan the transaction or exchange before it takes place. Such planning will cover:

- what is required from both parties (definition of performances);
- what happens if a party does not do what it is supposed to (effect of defective performances or non-performance);
- what happens in unforeseen circumstances (effect of contingencies beyond the control of the parties);
- what happens if things go really wrong (whether legal sanctions will or will not be used).

Most contract law is case law rather than statute. This means that virtually everything is subject to interpretation. So there appears to be, for example, no clear answer to the question of whether a grant or a service agreement is or is not a contract.

Convergence and divergence

Sociologists have recognised that in a contractual relationship each party needs the other but often seeks to obtain what it needs at the lowest price (to acquire the most rights possible in return for the fewest obligations possible). The process of defining each party's rights and obligations is negotiation.

Contractual negotiation recognises a **convergence** of the parties' aims (cooperating for a common purpose) as well as **divergence** (seeking to achieve different or conflicting aims). The object of contract law is to achieve equilibrium between convergence and divergence.

What is a contract?

A binding contract comes into effect when there is an **agreement** between the parties, supported by a **consideration**, with the **intention** to create legal relations between the parties. These terms are described below.

Agreement

A **statement** during a contractual negotiation is an indication of what the **offeror** (the person making the statement) is willing to provide to the **offeree**. The statement might involve the services which an offeror is willing to provide, or the price an offeror is willing to pay for those services.

Negotiation involves a series of statements from each offeror to each offeree. In a contractual negotiation each party is both an offeror and an offeree; for example a voluntary organisation (offeror) says it will provide a service to the local authority (offeree); the local authority (offeror) says it will pay a certain amount to the voluntary organisation (offeree).

An **offer** is a final statement in which the offeror indicates, by word or conduct, a willingness to enter into a binding relationship as soon as the offeree accepts the offer, without further negotiation. It can be difficult to distinguish between statements and offers!

The offeree may indicate that the offer is not acceptable, and may make a **counter-offer** indicating what would make the offer acceptable. If the offeree simply asks whether the offeror would be willing to change its offer, this is not in itself a counter-offer.

Agreement occurs when one party unconditionally accepts an offer made by the other. The terms of the offer itself may be full of renegotiation clauses, price variation clauses and similar conditions in order to allow flexibility. But the acceptance or agreement itself must not be subject to any conditions.

So agreement occurs if one party says, 'I agree to accept your offer, including the condition that after six months we will reconsider the price you will pay.' In this case, the condition is part of the offer. Agreement does not occur if one party says, 'I agree to accept your offer, on condition that after six months we will reconsider the price you will pay.' Here the condition was not part of the offer and is being tacked on as a condition of agreement.

The basis of the **contract** is agreement of both (or all) parties to the offer(s) made by the other party or parties.

Until an offer is accepted and that acceptance is communicated to the offeror, it creates no legal rights. Up until the point when the acceptance is communicated, the offeror may revoke or withdraw the offer, the offeree may reject the offer outright or make a counter-offer, or the offer may lapse if it is not accepted within a certain time.

Contract can also be viewed on the basis of **bargain**. A bargain exists when an offer is accepted and thus becomes a **promise**. A binding promise exists when an offer is made and accepted.

So when an offer is made and accepted, an agreement or a bargain has been made and a binding promise exists which must be fulfilled. This is the basis of the contract.

Consideration

Consideration is **anything of material value** which is offered by one party in exchange for consideration from the other party. In buying a television, the TV and the money paid for it are both consideration. In providing a service, the service and the money paid for it are both consideration. Contract law also regards **promises** as consideration, for example the promise to provide a service by a certain date.

Something wholly performed before a promise is made cannot be a consideration.

Intention

Not only must the parties reach agreement, but they must intend to create a legal relationship. This intention does not need to be explicitly stated, and does not even need to be the real intention of the parties to *this* agreement. 'It means that intention which reasonable parties would have had in those circumstances.' The court, rather than the people actually involved, decides whether intention exists in a particular agreement.

For a contract to exist:

- Each party must offer a consideration (goods, services, payment or the promise of any of these) to the other.
- Each party must unconditionally accept the terms under which the other party's consideration is offered.
- There must be an intention to enter into a legally binding relationship. But even if the parties say there is no such intention, a court could still rule that such intention existed.

Contracts do *not* have to be written, or in complicated legal language; they do not even have to be signed. But clearly it is easier to enforce a contract if it is written and signed than if it is unsigned or verbal.

The law usually presumes that business agreements are binding contracts, but that agreements of a social or domestic nature are not.

What does a contract include?

Scope of the agreement

Express terms (called this because they are explicitly expressed) define the consideration to be provided by both parties. This may be done in vague or very precise terms. Express terms may be written or oral.

Implied terms are not specifically stated as part of the contract but may be part of the contract anyway because they exist in statutes or business practice. If a court considers it necessary, it may imply terms. This might happen, for example, if a contract is badly written or if a standard form of contract is used which does not cover the particular circumstances of this contract.

In many contracts there is a middle ground where terms are not expressed verbally or in writing, and are also not implied. So a contract might say that an organisation is to 'provide community activities' without specifying what they are and without indicating how decisions will be made about what should be provided. This can seem advantageous, because it allows for flexibility. However it can create problems if there are disputes later about inadequate performance or non-performance.

Form of the agreement

Contract law is not generally concerned with the form of the agreement. It does not matter if a contract is written on a memo pad or on fifty pages filled with legal language, or even if it is not written at all. If an offer involving consideration has been made and accepted with the intention of creating a binding agreement, a contract exists.

Never, never, never agree to a contract without reading, understanding and thinking through the implications of every single term. If you don't understand what something means, ask for a straightforward explanation and keep asking until you get one.

You can use contracts from other organisations as models, but always adapt them to your particular circumstances.

Content of the agreement

Chapter 3 looked in detail at what a contract made by a voluntary organisation might include.

Letters of intent

A letter of intent (sometimes called an instruction to proceed) states that the sender intends to enter into a contract with the addressee. It is risky to start work on the basis of a letter of intent. The courts regard binding obligations as being created only if and when the parties actually enter into a contract.

However, if a contract is later created and there is a dispute about payment for work which has already been done, a court *may* say that the contract should operate retrospectively to the date of the letter of intent. And if a contract is not created, a court *may* rule that if work has been done and accepted it should be paid for at a reasonable rate. But these outcomes would require legal action.

Performance of the contract

Definition of acceptable performance

Terms which describe performance indicate what the contractual obligations are and how they will be fulfilled. They might also expressly indicate the required quality of performance. Often, however, required quality of performance is implied. This can lead to problems if the two parties have different ideas about what has been implied.

It is important for all parties to the contract to be clear not only about the required quality of performance, but also about how performance will be monitored, by whom, when, and against what criteria. This may be written into the contract itself or into an appendix or schedule attached to the contract, or it may be set out in correspondence.

Any indication of disagreement about whether performance is acceptable should be dealt with immediately.

Action for breach

A legal action for breach can be brought if one party fails to perform all or part of a contractual obligation, or performs it defectively (inadequately). The breach can apply to express terms (written or oral) or implied terms.

The basic remedy for breach is payment of **damages** to compensate the injured party for loss suffered as a result of the breach. A serious breach might lead to the right to **terminate** the contract.

To protect your organisation you should:

- Be sure management committee members know and understand what is in the contract.
- Be sure the organisation can meet all the terms in the contract.
- Be sure the organisation is receiving adequate remuneration for the work you will be obliged to carry out, including a full share of the overheads and any contribution to capital expenditure which is being undertaken.
- Discuss with relevant staff and committee members the quality of service you want to provide, and how that service couldbe monitored and assessed. Then negotiate and agree theseperformance indicators with the purchaser of services (thelocal authority, health authority etc). Don't let the purchaser define the performance indicators for you.
- The other party has obligations as well! Be absolutely clear about what you expect from them, when, and how it will be assessed.
- Keep up to date with good practice as it is developed for contracts in the voluntary sector. Subscribe to the free quarterly bulletin *Contracting - In or Out?* published by the Local Voluntary Action Department of the National Council for Voluntary Organisations (26 Bedford Square, London WC1B 3HU). If your organisation is involved with care in the community, get relevant publications from the Community Care Project at NCVO.
- At the first sign of any problem or disagreement, sort it out. It won't go away if you ignore it.
- If legal action is threatened, or if you feel you might have to take action against the other party to the contract, get specialist advice. Litigation can usually be avoided if the problem is dealt with sooner rather than later.

Responsibility for breach

If a voluntary organisation which has allegedly committed a breach is incorporated (as a company limited by guarantee, company limited by shares, or industrial and provident society), action for breach would be taken against the organisation itself. Any damages payable to the other party would be paid by the organisation. If the organisation does not have enough money to pay the damages or does not have appropriate insurance, it could (in a worst case scenario) go bankrupt.

If the organisation is not incorporated, the individual members of the management committee (and senior staff if they have management decision-making responsibilities) could be sued for breach. Indemnity insurance is available for such circumstances.

6. Charities and contracts

Charitable status and legal status

Regardless of whether it is incorporated or unincorporated (see Chapter 7), any voluntary organisation or community group may have **charitable status** if all of its objects and all of its activities are charitable as defined by law. The books listed in chapter 2 under 'Legal structures and charitable status' describe charitable objects and activities.

Many people do not realise that charitable status is *completely separate* from **legal status**. Legal status is defined by whether the organisation is registered as a company limited by guarantee, industrial and provident society, friendly society or trust, or whether it is an unregistered association (a club, society or any other group which is not registered). An organisation may have any of these types of legal status *and* have charitable status, or it may have any of these types of legal status and *not* have charitable status.

Charitable status has advantages, notably tax and rate relief, but it also has its limitations. This chapter considers some of the advantages and limitations as they relate to charities and contracts. When considering entering into a contractual relationship with a funding body, the most important advantage of charitable status is relief from taxes on profits; the most important limitation is on the right to trade.

Most organisations in England and Wales gain charitable status by registering with the Charity Commission. At the time of registration the Inland Revenue, which is responsible for granting tax-exempt status, will also give its recognition that the organisation is a charity.

A company limited by guarantee which is registered as a charity is called a **charitable company**. It will be registered not only with the Charity Commission but also with the Registrar of Companies, who is concerned to see that the organisation carries out its obligations as a company but has no interest in the charitable nature of the organisation.

A friendly society or industrial and provident society whose objects are charitable is an **exempt charity**; it gets the advantages of charitable status without having to register separately with the Charity Commission. The organisation registers with the Registrar of Friendly Societies, who has an overall supervisory role to see that the organisation is operating properly.

In Scotland and Northern Ireland there is no system for registering charities. Charitable status is obtained there by gaining recognition as a charity from the Claims Branch of the Inland Revenue.

Responsibility for charities

All registered charities have **charity trustees** who may (or may not) be the same as the management committee members. If the charity is also a company, the management committee members may be charity trustees *and* company directors.

If the trustee body is different from the management committee, the relationship between the two groups should be clearly set out in the organisation's constitution. If it is not included in the constitution, there should be a minute of a trustees meeting authorising the delegation of some responsibilities to the management committee and the terms under which such responsibilities will be undertaken.

The trustees always have ultimate responsibility for a charity, which can cause problems if the trustees and management committee members do not know what each other is doing or disagree about what the organisation should do.

Paperwork and administration

Charities are obliged to submit annual accounts to the Charity

Commission. These do not have to be independently audited unless the charity is also a company or an industrial and provident society (or if funding bodies require audited accounts). The new Charities Act (expected in 1991 or 1992) is likely to make an audit a requirement if the charity's annual income is above a certain level.

Advantages of charitable status

Tax and rate reliefs

Charities do not have to pay *income tax* or *corporation tax* on their profits. (But people who are employed by a charity have to pay income tax on their earnings from the charity, the same as on any earnings.)

Charities are not exempt from *VAT* but there are special exemptions for some services provided by charities and other voluntary organisations. Chapter 8 explains the basics of VAT, and additional information is available from any Customs and Excise office.

Charities do not pay *capital gains tax* on gifts they receive or on gains from the sale of their own assets.

In general charities do not have to pay *inheritance tax* on money left to them by people in their wills, but tax may be payable if there are any conditions attached to a bequest. Always get advice from a solicitor or accountant.

Charities get mandatory 80% relief on *non-domestic rates* for premises used wholly or mainly by them for charitable purposes. The rating authority may give discretionary relief on the remaining 20%. This relief applies to other voluntary organisations if all of their aims are charitable, even if they are not registered as a charity.

The rating authority may also give discretionary relief to other (non-charitable) voluntary organisations and non-profit organisations. The Department of the Environment has issued guidance on this which is available (along with much other useful information) in *Responding to Rate Reform: A guide to the poll tax and*

Local Government Finance Act 1988 by Jane Hutt (National Council for Voluntary Organisations, February 1990, £3 from Local Voluntary Action Department, NCVO, 26 Bedford Square, London WC1B 3HU).

Under the Rating Disabled Person Act, premises may be wholly exempt from non-domestic rates if they are used to provide training, welfare services or other activities for people with disabilities or for people who are or have been suffering from illness. Places of worship and church halls are also exempt. The rating authority can provide details.

Reclaiming tax paid by donors

A charity can reclaim from Inland Revenue the income tax paid by individual donors who give money under a four-year *covenant* or who give a one-off donation (*Gift Aid*) of £600 or more out of their taxed income. With basic rate income tax at 25%, this can increase the value of personal donations by 33%.

Under the Give As You Earn scheme employees and pensioners can authorise their employers to deduct from their pay a contribution to any charity. The employee does not have to pay income tax on any contribution made in this way. It is a painless way for employees to donate an extra amount to charities: if a person earns £10 and donates it to charity through GAYE the charity gets the full amount; if the person earns £10, pays income tax on earnings then gives what's left to the charity, the charity would get only £7.50. There is a limit of £600 per tax year (6 April to 5 April) on the amount which an individual can give in this way.

Corporate donors who give money under a four-year covenant or who give a one-off Gift Aid donation can offset the cost of their gifts against their corporation tax liability. For most companies there is a minimum level for a Gift Aid donation of £600, but a covenant can be for any amount. The company's donation has to be made after deduction of income tax at the basic rate, and this income tax can subsequently be reclaimed by the charity. The net effect of this is that the value of the gift is increased by one-third in the hands of the charity, and the company which has to pay over the income tax on the gift to the Inland Revenue (£200 on a £600 gift) will save itself this amount or more in corporation tax (depending on the rate at which it pays corporation tax).

Limitations of charitable status

The three main limitations of charitable status are the restrictions on involvement in politics and campaigning, restrictions on having employees on the trustee body, and restrictions on trading.

Politics and campaigning

Although charities cannot do anything which is overtly *party political*, the Charity Commission's advice on what they *can* do is often confusing. In general, 'political' or campaigning work by charities is acceptable if the issues are directly related to the charity's objects, and if the activity is ancillary to the charity's main work but has an obvious relationship to it. Charities can also provide educational information. If in doubt, you can seek advice from the Charity Commission.

A charity which is generally responsible but which strays into areas subsequently defined as non-charitable will lose tax reliefs on funds used for those activities, but will not lose its charitable status. The individual trustees could be asked to repay to the charity the money used for the 'political' activities, because it was a breach of trust for the money to be used in this way. But if the trustees have acted in good faith they will not be held liable.

Employees on the trustee body

Trustees of a charity cannot be employed by the charity, even for part-time or temporary work, unless this is expressly permitted by the organisation's constitution. Normally the Charity Commission will not register an organisation which permits its trustees to be remunerated as employees. Conversely, employees of the charity cannot be trustees and cannot be on the management committee if the committee is also the trustee body.

There are a very few exceptions to this; for details see pages 53-55 of *Charitable Status: A practical handbook* (see Chapter 2).

Charities and trading

Trading means charging for goods or services and/or being paid for them. Receiving a grant does not constitute a trading activity. Entering into a contract or similar legal arrangement may in some situations be classed as trading and may therefore be subject to restrictions on charity trading.

Primary purpose trading

If a charity provides goods or services which **directly further its primary objects** it can charge for them or be paid for them, and according to the Charity Commission this does not constitute 'trading'. The essential point is that the goods or services must fall directly within the primary purpose of the charity. This type of trading is known as **primary purpose trading**.

Note that even if the sale of goods or services is not classed as trading for charity or tax purposes, it can still constitute a business activity for VAT purposes; see Chapter 8.

Most charity constitutions prohibit 'permanent trading activities'. This prohibition does not apply to primary purpose trading.

A charge for goods or services may be made to the users themselves as a fee. Or a third party may be charged for the services; this is what happens with contracts. If all the services or activities to be provided under a contract fall directly within the charity's primary objects there is probably no problem in charity law about the charity taking on the contract.

One possible exception is where the charity's objects do *not* involve 'relief of poverty' *and* its services or activities are restricted solely to members of the charity or to another small group, rather than being available to the public. An organisation which fits this description may not be able to define its activities as 'primary purpose trading' even if they seem to fall within its objects; get advice from the Charity Commission. Note that relief of poverty means providing relief or support not only for people who are poor, but also for people who are ill, or elderly, or have a disability.

Other permitted trading

There are other situations in which the sale of goods or services is not classed as trading, although these are unlikely to affect contract arrangements.

Sale of goods produced by beneficiaries of the charity. A charity can sell goods produced by the actual beneficiaries (users) of the charity, for example goods made in a sheltered workshop. The money earned must go to the charity, not directly to the beneficiaries.

Incidental small-scale trading. This covers bazaars, one-off fundraising events, small-scale sales of Christmas cards or promotional items, and similar activities which are not substantial, not regular or permanent and not in competition with other traders. All the money earned must be used for charitable purposes.

There is no official definition of 'substantial' in this context but if trading contributes more than one-fifth of the charity's total income it would probably be classified as substantial.

Sale of donated goods. Sales of donated goods through jumble sales, thrift shops and auctions are considered to be converting the donation into cash, rather than trading. So this is considered to be fundraising rather than trading.

Rental income. If premises are rented out under a lease or other agreement the income is considered as investment income rather than trading income. (Check that the charity has the power to own property and to invest; this must be explicit in the governing instrument.) Charges for room hire are considered trading income, so are only allowed if they are incidental and small-scale.

Considering contracts

Clearly there is no problem if a charity enters into a contract to provide services all of which fall within its primary object(s). It may not be easy to determine whether a service or activity does fall within the primary objects; if you have any doubts, you should contact the Charity Commission for advice.

If some or all of the services to be provided do not fall directly within the charity's primary objects and are therefore not classed as permitted trading, the charity will have to set up a **separate trading organisation** to take on the contract.

Even if all the services fall within the charity's primary objects, it could be risky for the charity itself to take on a substantial contract. If the contract fails, the other (non-contract) funds of the charity could be at risk. So even if it is not legally required, it may be sensible anyway to set up a separate organisation to take on substantial contracts.

The separate trading organisation might be established as a **charitable** or **non-charitable** organisation. If it is charitable it will only be able to undertake trading activities which fall within its primary purpose, but this purpose might (or might not) be different from the primary purpose of the original charity. A non-charitable organisation will be able to undertake other trading. For example, a charitable meals-on-wheels service can only provide meals to people who are ill, disabled, etc. A non-charitable service could, if it wanted to, subsidise the meals-on-wheels service by setting up a catering service selling lunches to schools or local businesses.

A separate trading organisation does not have to be incorporated, but usually it will be. If it is not incorporated, the individual members of the management committee will be personally liable for any debts or responsibilities of the organisation. If the organisation is incorporated, the directors (management committee members) have limited liability if things go wrong financially. This is explained in more detail in Chapter 7.

If a charitable trading organisation incorporates, its legal structure will be either company limited by guarantee or industrial and provident society. A non-charitable trading organisation will usually become a company limited by shares. Legal advice is essential to ensure that the proper structure is chosen.

A charitable trading organisation is not supposed to trade primarily for profit. This means that in charging for its services or in pricing services under the contract, the intention must be to break even rather than to make a profit. But provision for inflation, replacement of equipment, improved services or development of its work can be built into the pricing, so it might end up showing a 'profit' at the end of the year. Because of the tax reliefs which charities get, no income tax or corporation tax will be payable on this profit.

But a charity whose activities are exempt from VAT (see Chapter 8) may lose this exemption if it builds into its costs provision for improved services or development. The exemptions are available only if the charity trades 'otherwise than for profit', and VAT regulations define 'profit' as anything more than costs plus overheads. Obviously the way you cost and price an activity is highly significant; this is explained in Chapter 9.

Any profit shown by a charity must be held within the charitable fund of the organisation and must be used for charitable purposes. The profit cannot be accumulated indefinitely. If profits are accumulated, both the Charity Commission (which is responsible for seeing that the charity's funds are properly applied) and the Inland Revenue (which is responsible for tax reliefs) will start asking questions.

A non-charitable trading company has no restriction on its profit-making. Any profit earned is usually transferred back to the charity in a way which ensures that no tax has to be paid on the profit.

Separate trading organisations

Parallel charitable trading company

If all the trading activities to be undertaken under the contract(s) fall within the charity's objects, the separate trading organisation could be a parallel charity with the same or similar objects and the same trustees as the existing charity, but with a different name. It would almost certainly be incorporated as a limited company.

The advantages of this arrangement are:

- The assets of the original charity are protected if anything goes wrong with the contract(s).

- The original charity can involve itself in advocacy without fear of directly jeopardising its contracts.
- Because the trading company is incorporated, the individual trustees have limited liability if anything goes wrong with the contracts.
- Both organisations get full tax and rate relief.
- The original charity can make grants or transfer funds to the trading company, and *vice versa*.
- The second charity is a separate body for VAT purposes. If neither organisation exceeds the VAT threshold (see chapter 8) neither will have to register for VAT, or if only one exceeds the threshold only that one will have to register.

The main disadvantages are:

- Both charities can only undertake primary purpose trading. This may limit the kind of work that can be undertaken under contracts.
- The finances of the original charity and the charitable trading organisation have to be kept completely separate, which means separate bank accounts, bookkeeping, audits etc.

Charitable trading company with different objects

If the services to be provided under the contract are all charitable as defined in law, but do not all fall within the primary purpose of the original charity, it might be possible to change the charity's objects to include the new ones. But this takes a long time and the Charity Commission might not allow it.

Another possibility is to set up a second charity with different objects. This has all the advantages listed above, except that the original charity can only make grants for activities undertaken by the second charity which also fit in with the first charity's objects (and *vice versa*).

Both charities can still only undertake primary purpose trading, but as the second charity will have been set up with its objects defined specifically for the proposed trade and any future plans, it may well be able to undertake a wider variety of activities.

A disadvantage will be the time it takes to set up the second charity, although this will probably be less than seeking to change the existing charity's objects.

Non-charitable trading organisation

If the charity wants to undertake substantial or permanent activities which are not charitable, it will have to set up a non-charitable trading organisation. As indicated above, this will usually be a company limited by shares.

Normally the shares in the company will be owned by the charity. If the charity's constitution explicitly permits it to invest and if the investment can be commercially justified, the charity will probably invest in the shares directly. In other cases, the shares will be purchased by a benefactor who will then make a gift of them to the charity.

A non-charitable trading company is not bound by charity restrictions so can undertake any trading activities, so long as they fall within the trading organisation's own objects.

In order to minimise its tax liability the company will pay most or all of its trading profits back to the charity under a deed of covenant, or donate the profits (if they are more than £800) annually to the charity under the Gift Aid scheme, or pay over the profits as a shareholder dividend. The trading company does not have to pay any tax on the profits which are paid back to the charity in any of these ways, and the charity does not have to pay any tax on the donation or investment income received from the trading company.

If the trading company retains any or all of its profits, it will be liable to pay corporation tax.

The idea of setting up a separate non-charitable trading company seems straightforward but there are many technical and operational difficulties. Because the trading company is not charitable it must be *completely separate* from the charity, so the following issues arise.

- Where will the trading company get its initial money from? It can come from the charity only if the charity has the power to invest in the shares of a private company.

- The charity can lend money to the company only if the charity has the power to do so, if the loan is 'reasonable' from a normal commercial standpoint, and if the Inland Revenue agrees to the loan.

- If the trading company has to borrow from a bank or commercial lender, the lender may want the charity to guarantee the loan or overdraft. This is a complex area; even if the charity has the legal power to provide the guarantee, the Charity Commission would probably not allow it to meet the guarantee if the trading company defaulted on the loan.

- The charity and trading company must have completely separate accounts: separate books, bank accounts and audits. This means extra time and expense.

- The charity must not in any way subsidise the trading company. Any use of the charity's premises, staff, equipment etc must be paid for at an 'arm's length' rate by the company.

- Some activities are exempt from VAT only if they are provided by a charity. So the company, which is non-charitable, would be liable for VAT.

- The end-of-year accounting can be tricky. If the trading company has covenanted all its profits to the charity or is making a Gift Aid donation of its total profits, the profits have to be paid to the charity before the end of the year, so the company does not show any profits in its EOY accounts. But how do you know before the end of the year how much the profits for that year will be?

- The money covenanted or donated back to the charity can be used only for charitable purposes within the charity's objects.

- It might seem sensible to covenant or donate all the profits to the charity, so no corporation tax is payable. But if none of the profits are retained by the trading company, how will it allow for inflation, contingencies or expansion? How will it build up reserves?

- There must be good communication between the governing body of the trading company (board of directors/management committee) and the governing body of the charity (trustees/management committee). (If the charity is itself a company, its trustees/committee may also be directors of the charitable company.) If the governing bodies involve the same people, they must be aware all the time of the separation between the two bodies.

- Not being charitable, the trading company will be affected by the provisions of the Local Government Act 1989 on 'local authority influenced companies' if one-fifth or more of the voting members of the company or its board of directors are associated with a local authority *and* the local authority is associated with half or more of the company's business (through contracts, grants, free rent etc). Chapter 7 explains this in more detail.

- Setting up a separate non-charitable trading company can require a great deal of staff and management committee time as well as expensive specialist legal and accounting advice. The time and costs must be budgeted for. This is separate from the substantial time and costs likely to be involved in tendering for and/or negotiating the actual contracts.

These are very complex issues and it is *essential* to get advice from a legal adviser and accountant who are specialists in this field.

Industrial and provident societies

An industrial and provident society is a voluntary organisation which carries out a business 'for the benefit of the community'. If all of its objects and activities are charitable it can enjoy all the benefits of charitable status.

At present the IPS structure is used primarily for housing associations and community businesses, but it is possible that it will come to be used for other types of voluntary organisation involved in permanent trading. The main disadvantage is that it can be expensive and time-consuming to set up an IPS which does not use a model constitution already approved by the Registrar of Friendly Societies.

For more information about IPSs contact the Registrar of Friendly Societies (15 Great Marlborough Street, London WC1, tel 071-437 9992) and ICOM (the Industrial Common Ownership Movement, Vassalli House, 20 Central Road, Leeds LS1 6DE, tel 0532-461738).

Before setting up a separate trading organisation:

- Read the chapter on 'Charities and money earning' in *Charitable Status: A practical handbook* (details in chapter 2).

- Look at your organisation's governing instrument (constitution, rules, or memorandum and articles of association). If it is written in legal language copy out the relevant sections and try to put them into plain English (it can be done!). If you are not sure what something means, make a note of it and ask for advice from a specialist or the Charity Commission. The most important sections are the objects (what the organisation was set up to do) and any powers relating to trading, investing and owning property.

- Consider whether all the trading activities to be undertaken fall within your present objects. If so, consider whether to set up a parallel charity; this is not necessary but may be advisable. If the trading activities do not fall within your present objects but are nonetheless charitable, consider whether to set up a charitable trading organisation with different objects. If the trading activities are not charitable, you will have to set up a non-charitable trading organisation. (Even if they are charitable, there can be advantages to setting up a non-charitable trading organisation.)

- Talk to your organisation's legal adviser. Ask if she or he feels able to advise you on this issue; if not, try to get a referral to someone else. The legal department at the National Council for Voluntary Organisations (tel 071-636 4066) should be able to advise.

- If you are considering setting up a non-charitable trading organisation, suggest that your legal adviser get a copy of 'Charities and trading' by Judith Hill and Jeremy De Souza, from *Trust Law and Practice* (vol.8 no.4, 1989, pp.98-103). This is a very clear explanation of some of the complex tax and charity issues involved in this sort of arrangement. For a reprint, send a stamped addressed envelope to the Directory of Social Change, Radius Works, Back Lane, London NW3 1HL.

- Meet with your organisation's auditor and talk through some of the financial issues outlined above.

If the charity decides not to set up a separate trading company, and if it is not itself already a charitable company, it should consider incorporation; see Chapter 7.

If the organisation does not have charitable status, it will have to pay corporation tax on any profits it shows in its end-of-year accounts. It should consider whether to set up a separate charity to which it can covenant some or all of its profits or donate its profits as Gift Aid.

Don't do anything without getting specialist legal and accounting advice.

7. Incorporation and contracts

Incorporation as a limited company or an industrial and provident society can, to some extent, protect management committee members from personal liability if a voluntary organisation gets into debt or other trouble. This chapter looks at the advantages and disadvantages of incorporation for organisations entering into contracts, and considers the implications of the Local Government Act 1989.

For any organisation which is incorporated or is considering incorporation, *A Practical Guide to Company Law for Voluntary Organisations* (see Chapter 2) is essential.

Legal structures and taxation

Legal structures for voluntary organisations are:

Unincorporated:

- Unregistered association, club or society
- Charitable trust
- Friendly society

Incorporated:

- Industrial and provident society
- Company limited by guarantee
- Company limited by shares

Any of these bodies (except a company limited by shares) can have charitable status (see Chapter 6) if its objects and activities are wholly charitable.

These legal structures, their suitability for various types of organisation and their advantages and disadvantages are explained in *Voluntary But Not Amateur* and in *Charitable Status: A practical handbook* (see Chapter 2).

Any organisation, regardless of whether it is unincorporated or incorporated, is liable to pay income tax or corporation tax on its profits unless it has charitable status, and it will not benefit from the tax reliefs available to charities unless it has charitable status.

Grants and donations are not classed as taxable income; trading and similar activities, rents from lettings, and interest and other investment income are taxable. If an organisation which does not have charitable status charges for its services or provides services under a contract and has money left at the end of the year, it will probably have to pay corporation tax on that money.

Any organisation, even if it has charitable status, must be registered for VAT if its turnover on non-exempt business activities (the value of the goods or services supplied during the year) exceeds the VAT limit (£25,400 in 1990-91). Grants and donations do not usually count towards turnover; income from contracts does. However certain business activities undertaken by charities, even under contract, will be exempt from VAT and thus do not count towards turnover for VAT registration purposes. Other activities undertaken by charities are zero-rated; these activities count towards turnover for registration purposes, and if the charity has to register for VAT it has to charge VAT on these activities — but at a rate of 0%. Chapter 8 explains VAT in more detail, and your local Customs and Excise office can provide leaflets on how VAT applies to charities and other voluntary organisations.

It is unclear whether service agreements, management agreements and similar arrangements count towards taxable income or turnover, but they probably do.

Being registered for VAT and having to charge VAT is not necessarily a bad thing. It allows you to reclaim the VAT you have paid on any purchases connected with a VATable activity, so can reduce your real costs. If you are being paid for services only by local authorities or other bodies which are registered for VAT, they will be able to reclaim the VAT they pay to you, so their real costs will not be increased.

Implications when entering into contracts

If an organisation which does not have charitable status enters into a contract it may find itself, for the first time, subject to corporation tax. If an organisation has charitable status and is therefore exempt from corporation tax, it may find that the limits on its right to trade may prevent it from entering into the contract! This is a complex area; read Chapter 6 and seek specialist advice.

An organisation entering into a contract may also find itself subject to VAT. If so, it must register with HM Customs and Excise as soon as its turnover in any 12-month period exceeds the VAT limit. Postponing registration can lead to a substantial fine.

Unincorporated associations

An unincorporated organisation does not have a legal identity of its own. In law, it is simply a collection of individuals. Unincorporated organisations cannot enter into contracts or other legal agreements in their own name. If they want to rent or buy property, employ people, borrow money or enter into any other type of contract, this has to be done (or will legally be assumed to have been done) by individuals acting on behalf of the organisation.

If an unincorporated organisation gets into debt or has other legal problems, the people who have responsibility for the organisation (the management committee, if there is one, or all the members) can be held personally responsible for the difficulties. They have **legal liability** for the organisation's debts.

This is probably not serious if the organisation is dealing only with relatively small amounts of money. But if it employs several staff, owns premises, or enters into complex contractual arrangements, management committee members are potentially taking on a heavy responsibility. In this situation, it is sensible to consider incorporation.

Incorporated associations

'Incorporate', from the Latin word *corpus* which means body, means 'to make into a body'. An incorporated organisation has an existence of its own, as a legal body separate from its individual members.

It can enter into contracts in its own name. If an incorporated organisation gets into financial or legal trouble, individual committee members are not personally liable unless they can be shown to have acted irresponsibly, negligently or fraudulently or outside their powers. Legally they have **limited liability.**

But under the **Insolvency Act 1986,** the directors (committee members) of an incorporated organisation may lose their limited liability if the organisation continues to trade (incur financial obligations) when there is not a 'reasonable' expectation that they will be able to meet the obligations. This is called **reckless** or **wrongful trading.**

Company limited by guarantee

Members of the company guarantee (promise) to pay a small amount, usually a nominal £1 or £5, if the company gets into financial trouble. So long as the company does not trade wrongfully, their liability is limited to this amount. Company members might be all the current members of the organisation, the founding members, or some or all of the management committee members.

A company's governing instrument is called the memorandum and articles of association. The memorandum sets out the organisation's objectives and what it can do (powers); the articles set out its rules and procedures.

It is not difficult to set up a company, and a ready-made company can be bought 'off the shelf' for a modest charge. But **don't use a model constitution without understanding what every section means and without carefully adapting it to your own organisation.**

If all of the company's objectives and activities are charitable, it can register as a charity. It is then a **charitable company** (see Chapter 6).

Paperwork and administration

A company secretary must be appointed (not elected) and is responsible for the considerable amount of paperwork involved: notifying the Registrar of Companies every time there is a change of company director, sending in an annual return and annual accounts, etc. Penalties are severe for the company secretary, all company directors (management committee members) and sometimes senior managerial staff if this paperwork is not done on time.

An annual return (not the same as an annual report) must be sent in within six weeks after the annual general meeting. An annual income and expenditure account and balance sheet must be prepared by an auditor in a specified form, and the annual accounts and annual report must be sent to the Registrar of Companies within ten months of the end of the financial year. Again, penalties can be severe if this is not done.

Industrial and provident society

This is a genuine cooperative, or a business or industry 'acting for the benefit of the community'. Co-ops of various types, housing associations and some community businesses are IPSs, but the structure is not used for many other types of organisation, probably because registration is expensive and slow if a model constitution is not used. Some voluntary organisations entering into contracts may find that this structure is appropriate; further information is available from the Registrar of Friendly Societies (15 Great Marlborough St, London WC1, tel 071-437 9992) and ICOM (Vassalli House, 20 Central Road, Leeds LS1 6DE, tel 0532-461738).

The constitution of an IPS is called its Rules and is generally less complicated than a memorandum and articles of association. An IPS must submit audited annual accounts, an annual report and an annual return to the Registrar of Friendly Societies, but the admin is less burdensome than for a company.

Company limited by shares

Very few voluntary organisations are set up as private companies with share capital. However, the structure may be appropriate if a charity which legally cannot undertake certain trading activities, wants to set up a **separate non-charitable trading company** to enter into contracts with a funding body. This is explained in more detail in Chapter 6.

A company limited by shares has even more paperwork than a company limited by guarantee.

Local Government and Housing Act 1989

The Local Government and Housing Act 1989 does not affect as many voluntary organisations and community groups as was originally feared. However it is complex and this section can only provide a general overview. As soon as the regulations for Part V of the Act are finalised, detailed information and guidelines about the Act will be available in *The Conduct of Local Government: A guide to the Local Government and Housing Act 1989* (£3 for voluntary organisations, £6 for others from NCVO Local Voluntary Action Department, 26 Bedford Square, London WC1B 3HU).

Local authority controlled and influenced companies

The Act affects an organisation *only* if it is a company or an industrial and provident society.

If the local authority controls more than half the votes at a general meeting of the company or IPS, the organisation is defined as a **local authority controlled company**.

If one-fifth or more of the voting members of the company or its board of directors (management committee members) are associated with the local authority *and* the local authority is associated with more than half of the company's business (through grants, contracts, free rent etc), then the company is a **local authority influenced company**.

A person is associated with the local authority if she or he is:

- a member of the local authority, or has been a member in the last four years; *or*
- an officer of the local authority; *or*
- an employee *and* an office-holder (director, manager, secretary etc) of a local authority controlled company.

Exemptions

At the time of going to press (October 1990) the regulations giving effect to exemptions from the regulations for voluntary organisations had not been published. However the Department of the Environment had assured NCVO that the following exemptions would be included.

There will be a **general exemption** from the regulations if a company or IPS meets *all* of these conditions:

- it is registered as a charity or all of its objects are charitable; *and*
- less than half its directors (management committee members) are associated in the local authority as defined above; *and*
- the local authority declares the company is independent; *and*
- the local authority declares it is not underwriting debt for the company.

If the company or IPS does not meet those general criteria, it can still have a specific exemption if *any* of the following apply:

- its grant from, or business association with, the local authority is £2,000 or less; *or*
- it is a registered housing association; *or*
- it is a building preservation trust registered with the Architectural Heritage Trust; *or*
- it is a member of an exempted national or regional network. NCVO's Local Voluntary Action Department has a complete list of exempted networks.

If the company does not meet any of the criteria for exemption it will be subject to various controls which apply to local authorities. In NCVO's view, the control which is likely to have the most impact is the control on borrowing. If a local authority influenced company wants to borrow more than £10,000 in a financial year or if it wants to increase its liabilities by more than £10,000 compared with the previous financial year, this borrowing will count against the local authority's own borrowing control total. The company will therefore have to obtain the local authority's approval. Given current restrictions on local authority borrowing, this approval might be difficult to obtain for large borrowings such as a mortgage.

When considering whether to enter into a contract:

- Look at your organisation's governing instrument (constitution). If it is written in legal language copy out the relevant sections and try to put them into plain English. The most important sections are those setting out the organisation's objects (what it was set up to do) and its powers.

- Be sure that the services to be provided under the contract fall within the organisation's objects, and be sure that the organisation has the power to enter into the contract. (Management committee members can be held personally liable if the organisation acts *ultra vires* (outside its objects or powers).

- If the organisation has charitable status, read Chapter 6 on charities and contracts. Consider whether it is necessary and/or appropriate to set up a separate trading company.

- If the organisation does not have charitable status, it will have to pay corporation tax on any profits it shows in its end-of-year accounts. Read Chapter 6 and consider whether to set up a separate charity to which it can transfer its profits as a charitable donation or by way of dividend.

- If the organisation is unincorporated (i.e. is not already a company or industrial and provident society), consider whether it should incorporate.

- If the organisation is already incorporated, consider whether it is necessary and/or appropriate to set up a separate company to undertake the contract.

- If the organisation is already incorporated, is thinking of incorporating and/or is thinking or setting up a separate company, consider whether it will be a local authority influenced company and the implications of this.

- Read Chapter 8, get the relevant VAT leaflets from Customs and Excise and consider whether the organisation will need to register for VAT. Discuss it with your auditor.

- Ensure that the organisation has good systems for financial planning and control, for keeping the management committee informed of the financial situation, and for financial decision-making. This is covered in Chapter 9.

Don't do anything without getting specialist legal and accounting advice.

8. VAT and contracts

The regulations for Value Added Tax are completely different from regulations for other types of tax. Corporation tax, for example, is a tax on profits, while VAT is a tax on the value of goods and services supplied, even if a profit is not made. Charities are exempt from corporation tax, but there is no blanket exemption from VAT for charities. Liability for VAT must therefore be considered completely separately from other tax issues.

Any local HM Customs and Excise VAT office (listed in the phone book under 'Customs') can provide general information about VAT, as well as specific leaflets for charities (701/1), clubs and associations (701/5), trade unions, professional bodies and learned societies (701/33) and youth clubs (701/35).

Other leaflets deal with specific activities and situations, some of which are applicable to voluntary organisations. Some of them are education and training (701/30), printed and similar matter (701/10), and catering (709/1 and 709/2).

All VAT leaflets are free. VAT regulations change quite frequently; always get up-to-date information from your VAT office.

This chapter emphasises the importance of investigating VAT as a part of the preparation for negotiating contracts. It explains how VAT operates and how it should be treated within an organisation's financial planning and bookkeeping procedures.

How VAT works

Registering and charging VAT

The provision of goods or services by *any* organisation or business is either **outside the scope of VAT** or is classed as a **business activity** for VAT purposes.

The goods or services provided in a business activity are called **supplies**. Some supplies are **exempt** from VAT. If a supply is not exempt, it is a **taxable supply**. Taxable supplies are taxed at **zero rate** (0%) or **standard rate** (15%).

Any individual, organisation or business which makes taxable supplies with a value of more than the current **VAT threshold** in any 12-month period, must **register** for VAT. When an individual organisation or business registers for VAT it is called a **registered person**.

The registered person must charge VAT on all the goods or services it supplies, unless the goods or services are exempt from VAT. The registered person is collecting the VAT on behalf of the government and must pay over the VAT it has collected to HM Customs and Excise every three months.

Paying and reclaiming VAT

Everyone — whether an individual, a business or an organisation — pays VAT on most goods and services which they buy. No one is exempt from having to pay VAT.

But if a business or organisation is registered for VAT, it can usually **reclaim** the VAT it has paid out. It does this by offsetting the VAT it has collected against the VAT it has paid out in the three month period. If it has collected more than it has paid out, it sends the difference to HM Customs and Excise; if it has paid out more VAT than it has collected, it gets a repayment from Customs and Excise.

An organisation which is not registered for VAT cannot reclaim the VAT it has paid out.

It sounds like any organisation in its right mind would register for VAT, so it can reclaim the VAT it has paid. You may find that you have no choice and have to register whether you want to or not. Even if you are not obliged to register it is worth considering whether to do so anyway, but you may find that you are not allowed to register or that the disadvantages outweigh the advantages.

Registering for VAT

The basic rule is that you must register for VAT and collect the appropriate tax from the people who pay for your goods and services if you are carrying on a business activity and your total supplies (sales of goods and services) in any 12-month period exceed the current VAT threshold (£25,400 in 1990/91). Even if you would not describe what your organisation is doing as a business activity, it would be classed as a business activity for VAT purposes unless it is defined as outside the scope of VAT.

Some supplies are exempt and do not count towards your total for VAT registration purposes. Other supplies are zero-rated; these do count towards the total when determining whether to register.

There are special rules which define some services as exempt when they are provided by charities or other voluntary organisations otherwise than for profit. These are described below, in the section on exempt supplies. 'Otherwise than for profit' means that the charge made for the goods or service (which might be a fee to the user, or a charge to a body such as local authority) is designed to do no more than recover the full cost, including overheads, of making this supply.

The VAT threshold figure applies to *any* 12-month period, rather than to a calendar year or your financial year. As soon as the value of your non-exempt supplies in any 12-month period reaches the threshold, you *must* register for VAT within the next month. Registration is not in itself complicated, but it will involve changes in your bookkeeping and financial reporting procedures.

VAT regulations as a whole are fairly complex; those relating to charities and voluntary organisations are no exception. It is important for *each* voluntary organisation to read the relevant leaflets, get advice from its accountant or auditor, and if necessary clarify its individual circumstances with its local VAT office.

If you fail to register and/or collect VAT when you should, your organisation may have to pay the tax from its own resources.

VAT on grants

VAT does not have to be paid on activities funded by donations, or funded by grants which are not earmarked for a specific purpose of some benefit to the donor. So a grant given for general purposes, or for a specific purpose which does not benefit the donor, is outside the scope of VAT and does not count for VAT purposes.

Grants or donations which are to be used for a specific purpose which 'will benefit the person making the grant' may be subject to VAT. So if you get a grant to provide services *on behalf of* a local authority, the grant could be subject to VAT.

In practice grants from local authorities to voluntary organisations have not normally been subject to VAT. But if you think that a particular grant could be subject to VAT, check with your accountant or auditor. If you are already registered for VAT or would be obliged to register as a result of obtaining the grant, the accountant will probably advise you to ask for the grant to be paid *plus* VAT. This will not in the long term cost the local authority any more, because it will be able to reclaim from HM Customs and Excise the VAT which it has paid to you.

VAT on contracts

Services provided under a contract will almost certainly be classed as business activities for VAT purposes, but may well be exempt from VAT. For charitable organisations exemption will depend on the nature of the goods and services provided, who the goods or services are provided to or for, and whether the business activities are being run 'for profit' or 'otherwise than for profit'. It is not your own judgement, or that of your funding authority or client, that matters in deciding whether something is a business activity liable for VAT or whether it is exempt from VAT; it is the judgement of the VAT inspectors. So **don't take risks about VAT** .

Sometimes it can be more advantageous for the activity to be chargeable to VAT, sometimes for it to be exempt. It is important to get proper financial advice and to sort this out *before* submitting the costing for a contract to the local authority or other potential purchaser.

If your organisation is not already registered for VAT, it will need to consider whether it becomes liable for registration as a result of taking on a contract. This will depend on whether the organisation's total income in any 12-month period from *non-exempt* supplies is more than the VAT threshold. Remember, it is not up to you to judge whether something is or is not exempt. Unless it *very clearly* falls within the exemptions outlined in the VAT guides, you will need to take advice from your accountant or auditor and the VAT office.

Voluntary registration

Even if your turnover is below the VAT threshold you may apply for voluntary registration, but only if your activities constitute a 'business' for VAT purposes. Before applying for registration you and your accountant or auditor should be convinced that registration will really be of value to you. If you register you will have to charge VAT on any goods or services you supply which are standard rated, and you will have to keep special financial records for VAT.

Charging VAT

All supplies of goods and services are classified into three categories: as supplies charged at the standard rate, as supplies charged at zero rate, or as exempt supplies. Most items supplied within the UK are standard-rated (currently 15%). Zero rating is not the same as exempt; the differences are explained below.

You can only charge VAT, even at zero rate, if you are registered to do so with HM Customs and Excise. Once you have registered you *must* charge VAT at the standard or zero rate on everything you sell (supply) unless it is exempt from VAT. You cannot pick and choose between clients; if you have to register because you are supplying services to your local authority's Arts and Leisure Department you will also have to charge VAT, where appropriate, to your users. This will not cost the local authority anything because it can reclaim the VAT it pays to you, but it will cost the users if they are individuals or organisations not registered for VAT.

Zero rate

Books, children's clothing, and certain supplies made to and by charities for blind people or medical charities are among the zero-rated items. The value of zero-rated supplies must be included in your totals (along with standard-rated supplies) when calculating whether you should register for VAT.

If you sell donated good in charity shops they can be zero-rated if the charity's primary objects are either the relief of distress or the protection or benefit of animals.

VAT is chargeable on zero-rated supplies, but at a rate of 0%. So if you are supplying zero-rated services or goods you will not have to charge anything extra to the individuals or organisations who pay for whatever you are supplying.

Because zero-rated supplies are VATable, you can reclaim the VAT which you pay out in the course of making those supplies. This is explained in the section below on reclaiming VAT.

Exempt supplies

A significant number of goods and services supplied by charities and other voluntary organisations are exempt *provided that* the charge (as fees to users or as a charge to another body) does no more than cover the cost, including overheads, of providing the goods or service. This is what is meant, in VAT terms, by making supplies 'otherwise than for profit'.

Welfare services provided by charities otherwise than for profit are exempt if they are for the 'provision of care, treatment or instruction to elderly, sick, distressed or disabled people' or for the protection of children and young people (see VAT leaflet 701/1). Education is exempt, as is training or retraining for a trade, profession or paid employment (leaflet 701/30). Provision for under-fives in places registered under the Nurseries and Child-Minders Regulation Act 1948 is exempt.

No VAT is chargeable on exempt activities and any income for them is not added into your total when considering whether you have to register. Because you cannot charge VAT on exempt supplies, you cannot generally reclaim the VAT which you pay out in making those supplies.

Even if your organisation is a registered charity, its activities are not exempt from VAT unless they fall into a specific exempt category or a category which is outside the scope of VAT. In borderline cases, the local VAT office will decide the VAT status of the activity.

If some of your activities are exempt and some are not, you will have to register for VAT if the value of non-exempt supplies exceeds the threshold.

Income from non-business activities

As already explained, donations and grants for general purposes do not count as business activities and are therefore outside the scope of VAT.

If you consistently provide goods or services *below cost* to 'distressed persons' for the relief of their distress, these goods or services are classed as outside the scope of VAT. 'Relief of distress' includes supplies made to elderly people (aged 65 or over), people with physical or mental disabilities, people who are chronically ill, and people who are poor.

Subscriptions to clubs or associations are not considered as a business activity provided that the subscriber is only entitled to receive reports on the organisation's activities and the right to vote. If payment of a subscription entitles the subscriber to other benefits — such as newsletters, admission to events, or free advice — the subscription income will usually be subject to VAT if the organisation is not a charity.

Interest earned on deposits is not subject to VAT.

Input tax

When you are registered for VAT you can claim back any VAT charged on the goods or services you buy and use for supplying standard-rated and zero-rated supplies. (There are some exceptions to this, such as VAT on cars.) This is your **input tax** (because it is a tax on supplies brought into the organisation). You will need to be able to show evidence of all expenditure where you have incurred input tax; you will therefore need to be rigorous in obtaining and keeping VAT receipts, which show the supplier's VAT number, for all purchases. Ordinary till receipts are not usually acceptable as VAT receipts.

If you provide exempt as well as standard-rated or zero-rated services, you cannot generally reclaim the VAT you have paid on goods or services specifically related to the provision of the exempt supplies. But there are some concessions which allow smaller organisations to reclaim all their input tax even if some of it relates to exempt supplies. If you provide exempt as well as standard-rated and zero-rated supplies, you should read VAT leaflet 706 on partial exemption, and get advice from the VAT office and your accountant or auditor.

If you are setting up a new organisation special arrangements can be made to recover input tax on the costs of setting up. If you think this might apply, it is important to get VAT receipts for all setting-up costs.

Output tax

When charging your clients, users or customers for standard-rated goods or services you calculate the charge excluding VAT, then add the appropriate VAT. This is called **output tax** (a tax on supplies going out of the organisation). Although this money comes into the organisation it is not your money; you are merely collecting it for the government.

If the purchaser of your services is registered for VAT, they will be able to reclaim the VAT you are charging them, so the VAT has not added to their costs. But if the purchaser is not VAT registered (for example, if it is a small organisation with a VATable turnover under the threshold, or if it is an individual) the imposition of VAT will increase the real cost of your services to them.

The paperwork

Bookkeeping

To reclaim VAT you will need to create a separate column or account within the expenditure section of your bookkeeping system. Into this you post (enter) the VAT amount on any invoice you pay and on all cash expenditures, rather than including it as part of the cost of the item. This VAT input tax should not be included as part of your costs, since you will get this money back from HM Customs and Excise.

Although VAT which you have paid should not appear as a cost in your income and expenditure account, it should remain in your cashflow projection as a part of the money you have to pay to your suppliers. You should calculate the costs of your operation on prices which exclude input VAT. (These processes are explained in chapters 9 and 10.)

Output tax — the VAT you charge to those who pay for your services — must also be isolated in your bookkeeping system and must not be added into the income in the income and expenditure account.

All invoices which you issue must show your VAT registration number, and all invoices or receipts for supplies which you purchase must show the VAT registration number of the supplier.

VAT returns

At the end of each three-month VAT period you have to complete a VAT return stating the total output tax you have charged and total input tax you have been billed for. You deduct the value of the input tax from the output tax and send the difference to HM

Customs and Excise. This is due one month after the end of the VAT period.

If your input tax during the period was greater than your output tax, you will get a refund from the VAT office.

For organisations with a turnover of less than £250,000 per year there is a special **cash accounting scheme** which lets you base your VAT payments on the actual output tax you have received and input tax you have paid during the period, instead of basing it on what you have charged (but perhaps not yet received) and what you have been billed for (but perhaps not yet paid).

On your cashflow projection the input tax must be included in the period when you expect to pay your suppliers, and output tax should be included when payments from customers are expected. You must also add in the net payment to Customs and Excise at the point where your return is due.

If your organisation's income from any sources in any 12-month period is more than the VAT registration threshold (£25,400 in 1990-91), think about the VAT implications.

- Any money which comes from donations or from grants which are not earmarked for a specific purpose of benefit to the donor are not classed as business activities so do not count towards the VAT threshold.

- Goods or services supplied under a contract are very likely to be defined as business activities. Unless the goods or services are exempt from VAT, income received under the contract will count towards the VAT threshold. If the organisation's income is thus above the threshold, it will have to register for VAT and charge VAT on the services it provides.

- Some important exemptions are 'welfare supplies' made by charities, education, training or re-training for employment, and under-fives provision in registered places. These supplies are exempt only if they are made 'otherwise than for profit', in other words if any charge made for them is designed only to recover the cost of providing the service. Exempt supplies do not count towards the VAT threshold, and you do not charge VAT on them.

- Interest on deposits is exempt from VAT and does not count towards the threshold.

- Subscriptions do not count as business activities provided the subscription gives the member nothing more than the right to vote at general meetings and/or the right to receive the organisation's financial accounts and reports on its activities. Such subscriptions do not count for VAT.

- Subscriptions which give other benefits to members may count towards the VAT threshold and may be liable for standard rate or zero rate VAT. The rules are different for charities and non-charities. Calling a subscription a 'donation' does not make any difference; the main points are whether the organisation is a charity, and whether the subscriber/donor receives benefits in return for the payment.

- Don't be afraid of VAT. The paperwork is fiddly, but VAT registration has advantages, because you can reclaim the VAT you pay.

9. Financial planning and control

Financial planning is essential for two main reasons:

- to establish whether and how a proposed activity can operate viably (how it can generate enough income to cover the full operating costs or to cover the costs minus funds available from other sources);
- to provide a base against which actual financial performance can be judged and controlled.

Financial planning and control are always important, but in the contract culture having a budget and sticking to it takes on an added importance. Organisations will be legally obliged to meet contract specifications; if this cannot be done within the prices charged under the contract, the extra costs will have to be subsidised by other parts of the organisation (see Chapter 10, on costing and pricing).

Financial recordkeeping (bookkeeping) and reporting (management accounts) are of equal importance as a base for ongoing management decision-making, for maintaining security, and for accountability to members and funders. Financial control of contracts may require new and more complex systems, but if the organisation's existing procedures are good they can almost certainly be adapted to meet any new requirements.

For a comprehensive overview of financial management, *Financial Planning and Control: A practical guide* and *Accounting and Financial Management for Charities* (see Chapter 2) will be helpful. This chapter provides a basic introduction to the financial procedures which will need to be implemented in moving towards contracts.

Financial planning

Many voluntary organisations have been accustomed to drawing up their budgets on a fairly *ad hoc* basis. If their expenditure was more than anticipated, they went back to the funding agency for top-up, or they might put some extra effort into fundraising or, possibly, cut back on services.

With contractual arrangements organisations will have to be much more rigorous about financial planning, because they will be obliged to provide the defined services within agreed costs. If they fail to do so there may be financial penalties; this has cost implications as well as a consequent loss in credibility.

The process of preparing a business plan or financial plan involves estimating all elements of cost that you expect to incur in the proposed activity, and estimating the likely income. Making these estimates requires research, and probably a series of decisions about precisely how the activity will be undertaken, to produce a set of **assumptions** upon which the plan is based. So the process is an excellent way to recognise and resolve the main issues surrounding the proposed activity and how it will be run.

In preparing a business or financial plan it is important to be realistic about what can be achieved. Be cautious about potential income, and take care not to underestimate your costs. When you have produced a plan on this basis you can take a second look at the assumptions, and make adjustments where they can be justified. But beware of 'fiddling the figures' just to make the plan look good.

Like many specialist fields, finance has developed its own language. This tends to mystify activities which many of us carry out quite happily in our private lives; it can also cause confusion if people use terms in different ways. So in the next section some basic terms are explained.

The language of financial planning

Budget and cashflow projection

A **budget** is a list of all the anticipated expenditures and incomes for the proposed activity or activities over a stated period of time. It has the status of a statement of intent: what the organisation wants to do, what it expects to happen. A budget usually refers only to money transactions, but can be extended to include non-monetary transactions such as gifts to be made in kind or the value of volunteers' time.

A **cashflow projection** shows when money has to be paid out, and when it is likely to be received. In effect it spreads the budget across smaller time periods, usually month by month though if money is expected to be very tight it could be week by week. To produce a cashflow projection you will have to make assumptions about when money will come in and when it will have to be paid out.

In financial planning the cashflow projection is important because the bottom line — the **surplus or shortfall carried forward** at the end of each period in the projection — predicts how much money you will have at the end of the period. This gives an early warning of possible cash shortages. If the expenditure planned for the period is going to be possible the predicted shortages will have to be overcome. This might be done by, for example, arranging a loan, reducing expenditure, holding payments over until a later period, or increasing income.

The money needed to maintain a cash surplus is the **working capital requirement**. Working capital is the amount of money (in cash and borrowing capacity) which is required to meet the financial commitments of the organisation or operation. The need for working capital arises because money has to be paid out (for example to purchase raw materials, pay for goods or services, pay wages, run premises and operate vehicles) before payments are received from customers or purchasers.

Receipts and payment account

The simplest form of account is a **receipts and payments account** (R&P account) which shows the amounts of money coming into the organisation (receipts) in a stated accounting period and the amounts going out (payments) in the same period. The difference between the money which has come in and the money which has gone out is the cashflow.

A projected R&P account shows the money you expect to receive and pay out within the stated period.

An actual R&P account shows movements of money (cash, cheques, bank transfers etc) that actually took place in the period.

Receipts and payments accounts are usually used only by small organisations.

Income and expenditure account

The movements of money shown in a receipts and payments account usually relate to payments for goods or services. But often payment is made in one financial period, and the goods or services are actually *provided* during a different financial period. Some examples of this are:

- grants received in advance for work to be done over an extended period;
- goods or services purchased or sold on credit, where payment follows later;
- goods or services which have to be prepaid, such as telephone rental;
- goods that are produced or bought in now, but used or sold at a later date (stock);
- large non-consumable items where the cost should be spread over many accounting periods through depreciation.

The accounting convention (standard procedure) is to include in the accounts for any one period only the incomes and costs which relate to that period. So even if you actually pay your next quarter's rent in September, an accountant would not expect it to appear in your accounts in September. It would be shown in the accounts as one-third paid in October, one-third in November and one-third in December.

When a receipts and payments account is adjusted for these time lags, it produces an **income and expenditure account** (I&E account). Unless an organisation's financial dealings are very simple, an I&E account is most appropriate for financial management. In commercial companies, an I&E account is also referred to as a **profit and loss account**.

Terms used in I&E accounts are **creditors** (people you owe money to), **debtors** (people who owe money to you), **accruals** (money you have received for goods or services you have not yet provided) and **prepayments** (money you have paid out for goods or services you have not yet received).

In financial planning it may be appropriate to include a projected I&E account. It may be useful to divide this into relatively short operating periods (perhaps one month or one quarter) as a basis for monitoring actual performance.

Balance sheet

The elements of a financial plan described above all cover a *period of time*. The final element in the financial plan, the **balance sheet**, is a statement or picture of the organisation's financial value at a *particular point in time*.

It includes the organisation's **assets** (premises, equipment, money in the bank and held as petty cash, stocks, money owed to the organisation, and money which the organisation has paid out in advance of actually receiving the goods or services paid for) and its **liabilities** (loans to the organisation, money invested in the organisation, money owed by the organisation, and money paid to the organisation for goods or services it has not yet provided).

Subtracting liabilities from assets produces a **net value** for the organisation at that point in time.

The final section of the balance sheet sets out the source of funds, showing how the net value has been funded. This might typically include the accumulated surpluses left over from earlier years, grants and gifts, loans and (for trading companies) shares issued by the company.

Depreciation

Most of an organisation's expenditure is usually on running costs (salaries, rents, admin expenses etc) or on goods which will be used up within the next year or so (stationery, food, newsletters etc). This expenditure is simply shown in the accounts, adjusted for any time lags as indicated above. But when you purchase equipment, vehicles or premises that will be used over a period of years, you consume or use up the value of the asset over a number of years. This is reflected in the accounts by a process called **depreciation**.

This is done by holding the value of the asset in your balance sheet and charging a portion of the cost to your I&E account each period. Depreciation applies only to **capital expenditure** (premises, premise renovations, vehicles, and items of major equipment which will last more than a year). Depreciation does not apply to small items like calculators and telephones, whose value is written off in the accounts as it is incurred.

Different items will be depreciated over different lengths of time, depending on their 'useful life'. The charge will be the total cost divided by the number of accounting periods during the 'life' of the item.

This means that large items of capital expenditure do not appear as expenditure in the I&E account, which would distort the financial picture by showing an unnaturally high level of expenditure for that financial period. But they do still appear in the cashflow, because they will have to be paid for at the time of purchase, and not over their projected life. Your accountant will advise you on appropriate time periods for depreciation.

Reserves

You may choose to create **reserves** or **provisions**, which is a way to save for the replacement of a capital item when the existing item has reached the end of its useful life, or for large items of expenditure which you know are going to have to be paid for in future. In each accounting period, a charge is made to the I&E account and a corresponding credit shown on the balance sheet. This is just a paper transfer and will not appear in the cashflow.

Some basic accounting definitions:

- The **budget** (or projected receipts and payments account) shows how much income and expenditure you anticipate for a financial period.
- The **cashflow projection** enables you to predict and plan for cash shortfalls.
- The (actual) **receipts and payments account** shows how much money you actually paid out and received in a financial period.
- The **income and expenditure account** is an receipts and payments account adjusted to include all transactions which relate to the particular financial period, even if the money doesn't actually change hands during the period.
- A **balance sheet** shows the financial worth of the organisation on a fixed date.
- **Depreciation** is a process for spreading the cost of capital items across all the accounting periods during which you will be using the items (on paper only — not in reality).
- **Reserves** are money held back to replace capital items or for other specific purposes.

Putting together a financial plan

To put together a financial plan for an activity, you start with a budget and cashflow projection, since these summarise the money needed to start and operate an activity, and the likely income and expenditure once it is running. These can be easily explained to non-specialist workers and management committee members, and will enable them to participate effectively in the decision-making about an activity.

If the intention is to undertake a new activity, or to develop an existing activity in a new way, then a budget and cashflow should be done for the activity on its own (to identify the resources needed, the cashflow implications and the likely surplus or deficit), and then again for the whole organisation with the new activity included.

The budget should include **capital expenditure** (one-off spending on buildings, vehicles or equipment), **revenue expenditure** (operating costs) and **setting-up costs** (exceptional revenue costs incurred in setting up the activity, such as consultancy, staff recruitment and/or training, legal costs, or initial stocks). If the organisation undertakes two or more separately funded or separately costed activities, the budget for each should also include a reasonable contribution to the general **management costs** of the organisation. These might include, for example, office and admin costs, supervision costs and the costs of servicing the management committee.

Careful research is needed to ensure that estimates are as accurate as possible. Concentrate your research effort on the biggest items of expenditure, and on sources of income. An assumption will also have to be made about a likely starting date and an allowance for cost inflation will need to be built into your projections, although these extra costs may in fact be covered by inflation in any charges to be made for the supply of the service. Also explore the implications of VAT (see Chapter 8); if you intend to register for VAT, the VAT on some of the setting-up costs can be set against subsequent income.

At this point the budget should, ideally, be showing a surplus which is at least sufficient to cover the depreciation charges on the capital items.

Next you will extend the budget into a cashflow projection. For each item think about when you will actually need to spend the cash, or when you can realistically expect to receive income. This will involve making assumptions about when you will hire staff and their terms and conditions, as well as assumptions about which suppliers you will use, when purchases will be made and whether you can negotiate credit terms with the suppliers.

You will also have to make assumptions about the terms that your customers or users will expect. Remember that many public authorities are very slow payers, and if you are reliant on a small number of large purchasers the regularity and timing of their payments is most critical. You may need to adjust potential income downwards to allow for possible bad debts.

It is helpful to do separate cashflow projections for capital and revenue items. From the latter a working capital requirement can be produced.

A series of difficult questions must now be faced:

- How will the operation be financed and what are the implications of this financing on the budget and cashflow? The interest charges attached to borrowing money must now be added into the budget, and the payment of interest and repayment of capital must be built into the cashflow.

- Is the operation viable? Is the organisation as a whole viable if this new operation is included? You must look at these questions in relation to both the income and expenditure and the cashflow. If there is a budgeted deficit in the immediate future how long will it be before a break-even is achieved? How certain are you that the projected break-even point will be achieved? Can you fund the operation until that point? Now is the point to start 'tuning' the proposed operation so that it produces a better financial projection, but remember that you are adjusting the proposed operations, not just the figures!

If you have to raise money from banks or other financial institutions you will probably have to convert your budget and cashflow to a set of **projected accounts** as part of your **business plan**. These accounts usually include a cashflow for each year until the operation reaches viability (when it is covering its costs and producing a sufficient surplus to cover depreciation costs and repay loans etc), and a projected income and expenditure account and balance sheet for each year of operation until this point. This is a more technical task and is best undertaken by someone with appropriate financial training.

Financial control and decision-making

Budgets and cashflow projections show how much income you need to cover projected costs, and when you need to receive that income. A receipts and payments account tells you how much money you have received and spent, and an income and expenditure account and balance sheet together give you an accurate picture of the organisation's financial status at any point in time. How can all this financial information be best used for monitoring the financial situation and making decisions about how the activity should be run and the organisation's financial future?

These projections and accounts are an essential **management tool for assessing the performance of the operation**. An analysis of the variances between projected accounts (for a month, quarter, year) and the actual accounts can identify key areas for management attention.

Your organisation should already have in place a working system for financial recording (bookkeeping), reporting (monthly, quarterly and annual accounts) and decision-making. Such systems become even more critical where grants are replaced by contracts and somewhat unclear legal responsibilities are replaced by clear legal requirements. This is especially important if payment is on the basis of performance, for example based on the number of units of output delivered, or if there are several contracts in operation and the survival of the organisation depends on achieving the projected levels of income and expenditure on each of them.

The **frequency** and **scope** of financial reports can vary. Preparing these reports consumes time, and that means cost, so it is important to assess what information is essential and concentrate effort here. As a guide, focus on the elements where variances will have most impact on the surplus or deficit produced or on the cashflow position. These will tend to be items which generate large figures (income for services provided, wages etc.) and are the most likely to fluctuate.

Analysis of variances

To understand the impact of figures it is useful to compare actual income or expenditure with the financial projections and undertake an **analysis of variances**. A typical report on expenditure might be set out like this:

Item	Actual £	Budget £	Variance £
Wages & NI	2300	2000	(300)
Rent	200	200	-
Telephone	500	330	(170)
Stationery	30	150	120
Materials	1500	1700	200
Heat & power	810	800	(10)
Transport	670	700	30
TOTAL	**6010**	**5880**	**(130)**

The figures show that overall expenditure is £130 more than budgeted. Wages and telephone are substantially over budget; stationery and materials are substantially under budget; the other items of expenditure are more or less on target. (The over-budget figures are in brackets to show that they are a deficit to the organisation. If we were looking at income, any variances where income was *less* than budgeted would be in brackets.)

Using variance analysis you would seek explanations for why there were differences between the budget and actual figures, especially for large variances like £300 over budget on wages and £170 over budget on telephone. Variance analysis is not a complex technical process; it is finding the answer to a simple one-word question: **Why?**

As the example shows, a **bottom line** which is quite close to the budget figure can conceal a number of significant cost over-runs.

The figures shown here are for a single period. A second set could be produced showing cumulative budget, actual and variance figures for a number of reporting periods, such as the 'year to date'.

It is easier to produce reports if the financial records (bookkeeping systems) are set up using the same headings as the budget and the financial reports.

If the activity or organisation has significant levels of debtors (people who owe it money), creditors (people it owes money to), stocks (of raw materials or goods for sale) or work in progress (products which are partly made but not yet completed as stock), it is important to adjust the receipts and payments for the period and produce an income and expenditure account and balance sheet as a part of the financial report. If you simply use the receipts and payments account as the basis for reports, showing only money actually received or paid out during the financial period, large variances are likely to occur from month to month, and it is virtually impossible to get an accurate picture of what is happening.

Producing an I&E account and balance sheet will require a higher level of accounting skills than other financial reports. This may require a regular input from the organisation's accountants. If this is necessary, it will need to be budgeted for.

If these are not to be produced on a regular basis but the operation does include significant levels of stock, creditors or debtors, statements of the value of these items should be included in the regular financial reports. If projections are made about what each of these will be at the end of the financial period, variances between the projected and actual figures can be analysed.

10. Costing and pricing

Costing is working out how much it will cost you to provide a service, run an activity or produce goods; **pricing** is working out how much you will charge for the service, the activity or the goods. For a voluntary organisation involved in contracts, the price is what the contractor (the voluntary organisation) charges the purchaser (the local authority, health authority etc) and the cost is how much the voluntary organisation has to pay to provide the service.

The difference between the cost and the price is the surplus (if price is higher than cost) or the deficit (if cost is higher than price). There is nothing intrinsically wrong in seeking to generate a surplus or make a profit. A surplus will guard against risk, enable you to enhance the service or provide funds to set aside for other work or towards the organisation's future. However, charging a price which does more than cover the costs of providing the activity may have implications for VAT (see Chapter 8).

Even if you do not seek to generate a surplus, you will want to ensure that you do not generate a loss or deficit on the activity. Any such deficit will have to be covered by the organisation's own funds or by another funding source.

A good financial plan (see Chapter 9) enables you to predict the cost of the activity. With an awareness of the projected costs and a decision about the extent to which you want to generate a surplus on the activity, you can decide on a price. But there is a dynamic relationship beteen costing, pricing and what the purchaser is willing to pay. Prices may be crucial in determining the level of demand for the goods or services, and therefore the income shown in the plan. If you price too high you may not get the contract or may not get enough sales to cover your costs; if you price too low you may get the contract but may not be able to deliver the service within budget.

Before you start fixing prices you must be aware of your costs; to get at your costs you need to have sketched out a financial plan. There is no short-cut in this process.

Dedicated and non-dedicated costs

When costing an activity it is useful to think of dedicated and non-dedicated costs separately.

Dedicated costs are directly related to carrying out an activity, and are therefore often referred to as **direct costs**. Dedicated costs can be sub-divided into **fixed costs** which will remain fairly static, at least in the short-term, no matter how much of the activity is carried out, and **variable costs** which change in a direct relationship with the amount of the activity.

As an example, a welfare rights worker costs the same regardless of whether she sees 15 clients or 80 per day, so her salary is a fixed cost. She needs a telephone so the phone line rental is a fixed cost. But the number of calls she makes varies with the number of clients she sees, so the phone usage costs are variable.

Non-dedicated costs, sometimes referred to as **indirect costs** or colloquially as **overheads**, are those which are shared by several activities. These might typically include the salaries of managers and administrators who service several activities, other administrative costs, publicity and public relations, audit and bank charges, insurance, and property running costs. All of these are likely to be 'fixed' in the short term.

Allocation of non-dedicated costs

If an organisation carries out only one activity or type of work, all costs will be allocated to that activity. But for organisations which carry out more than one activity, a critical part of costing is choosing an appropriate basis for allocating non-dedicated costs. This can play a crucial part in making the proposed activity appear viable or unviable, and will also have significant effects on the prices charged for specific contracts.

It can also be a highly political process. The tax-avoidance activities of large companies are based on varying the way that non-dedicated costs are charged to different operations and in different countries; and disputes about the viability of a product or service (for example between a trade union and management) can arise because of different beliefs about the appropriate way of distributing these costs.

In a voluntary organisation, for example, perhaps the social services department will be paying for some activities and the health authority for others. 'Political' choices will have to be made about how much of the rent, administration costs and other indirect costs are charged to each agency. If social services is making swingeing cuts this year, it may be wise to try to charge more of the indirect costs to the health authority. But what if the price is then so high that the health authority looks elsewhere for the service? This is all part of the process of costing and pricing the activity.

In sharing the non-dedicated costs between different activities the aim should be, in the first instance, to allocate costs so that each activity pays for what it uses. This can often be achieved by finding a suitable **measure** which can be applied to each activity. Within any organisation, even quite a small one, there might be several such measures. For example:

This type of cost:	might be allocated on the basis of:
Rent, electricity, maintenance	Square footage of space occupied by each activity
Wages administration, personnel costs	Annual wages cost of each activity
Finance and audit costs	Annual sales value or annual cost of each activity

Unit costs

One of the key features of the change to contract funding is a tighter specification of the services which are to be provided. In many cases this will require some means of specifying **units of provision** such as the number of person-hours spent in advice sessions, the number of residents to be cared for in a residential setting, the number of meals-on-wheels to be provided, the number of hours of operation of a leisure centre, or the numbers of users of a service.

An important prerequisite of contract negotiations is therefore to know your cost per unit of provision (**unit cost**). In doing these sums it may be useful to calculate the unit cost for the different elements of cost (dedicated variable, dedicated fixed, and non-dedicated) independently, and add them to produce a total unit cost.

In the short term the dedicated variable cost per unit does not change even if the number of units changes. But the unit cost of the dedicated fixed cost and the non-dedicated cost varies with the scale of operation. For example if dedicated fixed costs and non-dedicated costs are calculated as £10,000, and 10,000 units are provided, the unit cost is £1. But if only 2000 units are provided, the unit cost rises to £5.

Break-even

The **break-even point** for an activity is where total income is equal to total cost, including non-dedicated costs. The break-even point becomes important if you are to be paid according to the number of units of provision rather than as a block amount.

In this situation the break-even point is the level of provision you have assumed when dividing total fixed costs to find a unit cost. If you subsequently operate at a lower level of provision (perhaps for reasons beyond your control), you will make a loss because you will not be able to cover the fixed costs.

Operating at a higher level of provision will generate a surplus (profit) in financial terms. However this might have costs in management terms, such as overworked staff or over-use of equipment.

A cost **break point** is not the same as break-even point. It is the point beyond which level of provision cannot increase without an increase in fixed costs. Your advice worker, for example, gets the same salary whether she sees 25 or 60 people per week. But she simply cannot see more than 60; if you want to provide a service to 61 people per week you will have to hire another worker. Your small cooker can cope with cooking meals for 15 people each lunchtime; if demand increases you will have to get another cooker.

Assumptions

It is clear from the above that to establish the cost of providing any service or producing any goods it is necessary to make many assumptions. Most crucial of these are:

- How the provision or production is to be organised: the staff and equipment which will be required and the cost of these items.
- How much of the non-dedicated costs of the organisation should be paid for by this service or production.
- The level of provision or output which has been used to allocate the fixed costs (both dedicated and non-dedicated) to individual units of provision.

Under the terms of a contract, a voluntary organisation might be expected to provide a service at the same unit cost as a local authority or health authority is providing it. But in determining its unit costs, a local authority or health authority might be including only the dedicated or direct costs of providing that service. It might not be including substantial indirect or non-dedicated costs which are absorbed by other parts of the authority: staff recruitment costs paid for by the personnel department; wages administration, finance administration and audit charges paid for by the finance department; legal costs paid for by the legal department; building maintenance, grounds maintenance and vehicle maintenance paid for by the relevant departments.

An important part of costing and financial planning (especially where payment is linked to some measure of output or provision) is to ask some **'what if' questions** based on the big question: 'What if our assumptions are wrong?'

- What if the purchaser (local authority etc) won't pay for the share of indirect costs we have allocated to this contract?

- What if our costs rise sharply?
- What if inflation is higher than we have allowed for in our costings?
- What if certain elements of our costs are linked to factors beyond our control, for example salary costs linked to national wage negotiations, rents linked to rent reviews?
- What if the volume of output is lower than anticipated?
- What if the volume of output is higher than anticipated?

Changes in the assumptions upon which the plan is based will have an impact on the projected accounts and on the projected cashflow ... for both the individual activity and the organisation as a whole. They will play an important part in deciding how the activity is to be priced and whether the organisation wishes to submit a bid for the contract.

Pricing

It is important to understand the costs of providing a product or service *before* starting to price or tendering for work. However, the price charged need not be calculated on the basis of cost. A buyer who is in a powerful position (e.g. the main purchaser) may well tell potential suppliers what it is prepared to pay; the contract goes to the supplier who provides the best product or service for this price. On the other hand, a monopoly supplier may be able to charge prices which are many times higher than its costs (though probably wouldn't get away with this for long in the voluntary sector!).

An additional factor in pricing is the need to allow for a surplus (profit) to cover unexpected costs, development, equipment replacement, property refurbishment etc. But unless the organisation has charitable status and is carrying out activities directly furthering its primary purpose(s) as a charity, or is a non-charitable organisation covenanting its profits back to a charity, it may have to pay corporation tax on its profits. (See Chapter 6 for more about the tax benefits of charitable status.)

In deciding how much to charge for its services or goods, an organisation may choose from several **pricing strategies**, some of which apply only in very limited circumstances. Common strategies are:

- Cost plus: adding a fixed percentage to total costs.
- Penetration pricing: fixing a low price to establish the organisation, product or service in the market, then increasing prices.
- Promotional pricing: charging a low price for a limited period to attract customers.
- Marginal pricing: where the dedicated costs are covered and a contribution (but not the full contribution) is made to non-dedicated costs.
- Standard pricing: charging all customers the same price.
- Differential or variable pricing: charging different prices according to customer or client, region, order size etc.
- Price lining: charging the same price for similar products even if the costs are different.

Bear in mind that the price charged may have implications for VAT; some goods and services provided by voluntary organisations are exempt from VAT *only if* they are provided at or below cost (see Chapter 8). 'Cost' can include overheads, but it cannot include 'profit'.

The price charged may also have an impact on the demand for the goods or services being offered. This impact will depend on **price sensitivity**: how much does demand change if the price is increased or decreased? In the commercial sector demand for some goods or services is determined more by quality, design or delivery arrangements than by price; demand for voluntary sector services may be determined by quality, relationships with users or other factors rather than by price.

Issues for the voluntary sector

Voluntary organisations may find themselves in a rather special position: tendering competitively or negotiating a contract for services which have not previously been organised, costed or paid for on a quasi-commercial basis. Political and moral pressures may be exerted to try to ensure that voluntary organisations agree to deliver services on terms preferred by the purchaser authority.

In these circumstances it will be critical for the voluntary organisation to have made clear decisions about the appropriate cost of providing each service, and to be confident that it has the funds to cross-subsidise any contracts which generate incomes below break-even.

If anticipated income is insufficient to cover costs, beware of the temptation to plan arbitrarily for an increase in the price or in the volume of output to make the figures look OK. A solution may be possible by increasing sales; or it may require reductions in cost. Or no solution may be found: the activity may simply not be financially viable. In that case you will either have to fund it from a completely different source, or revise it substantially so it can cover its costs, or drop it.

If you are negotiating a price for a contract you may well have to rework several times the cost side of the budget and cashflow (hopefully reflecting different levels of service delivery) to come up with a package which meets the purchaser's requirements and users' needs, within the budget the purchaser is able and willing to pay, and in a way which covers your costs.

Some local authorities and other funders 'claw back' any portion of a grant which a funded voluntary organisation does not spend within the financial year. It is possible that they may try to do the same with services provided under contract. They may try to put a clause into the contract saying that if the voluntary organisation provides the services at less than the price charged, or covers some of the cost of the services from other sources such as fundraising events, then the local authority or other purchaser will 'claw back' the savings. This arrangement takes unfair advantage of the voluntary organisation, and removes the incentive to seek alternative sources of income.

11. Negotiating a contract

Negotiation is the process by which we get what we need or want from someone else. It may involve discussion, bargaining or haggling; whatever form it takes, it is an **interaction** between the parties.

In a negotiation, both parties want something, and both have something to offer. In barter each party is offering goods or a service which the other wants. In business negotiations one party is offering goods or services and wants to be paid for them; the other party has money and wants the goods or services. In personal negotiations what is on offer may be time, respect, security, independence, personal choices ('I want to stay at the disco till 3 a.m.' 'You're only 15 and I want you home by midnight'; 'I want to watch Rambo on TV' 'I want to watch Gone With the Wind'). Contract negotiations are the process of defining each party's rights and obligations.

Principled negotiation

Many people approach negotiations in a spirit of confrontation, winning points, achieving victory. In the short term this may seem successful to the side which gets what it wants. But even in the short term it may be unsuccessful, because it may alienate the other party so much that they go elsewhere for what they want. And any negotiation involving a long-term relationship between the parties is likely to prove unsuccessful if 'victory' is achieved by confrontation. The 'losing' side is unlikely to be committed to the outcome and may try to sabotage it in all kinds of subtle and not-so-subtle ways.

This approach to negotiation, seeing the participants as adversaries and the goal as victory, is sometimes called **hard negotiation**.

Soft negotiation is the opposite. Soft negotiators are people who want to avoid conflict at all costs, and who will agree to almost anything the other party wants in order to avoid disagreement or unpleasant discussions. Again, this may seem successful in the short term, because an agreed outcome is quickly achieved. But in the long term it is unlikely to be the best solution, and it may not be workable.

Roger Fry and William Ury, in *Getting to Yes: Negotiating agreement without giving in* (see chapter 2), advocate **principled negotiation**. In principled negotiation the parties are seen neither as adversaries nor as friends, but as problem-solvers looking at a situation in which both parties have needs and wants. The goal in principled negotiation is neither 'victory' nor 'agreement without conflict', but a **wise outcome reached efficiently and amicably.**

Principled negotiation starts not from fixed positions, but from a clear statement of what each party's interests, needs and wants are. It involves giving without giving in, and getting without grabbing. Far more than hard or soft negotiation it allows for creativity, new approaches and an outcome to which all parties are committed.

Fry and Ury offer four main guidelines for successful negotiation.

- **Separate the people from the problem.**
  The people you are negotiating with are neither enemies out to wreck you nor people whose friendship you have to cultivate. They are human beings there for the same reason as you: to negotiate the terms under which you will provide something that they are willing to pay for.

- **Focus on interests, not positions.**
  You are all interested in the best possible service for users and the community. Start from there, rather than from fixed positions about what you will and won't do.

- **Invent options for mutual gain.**
  Don't settle for options where you lose and they gain, or where they lose and you gain. You are in this together. Look for options which meet the needs of both parties.

- **Insist on objective criteria.**
  Judge the outcome of the negotiation not in terms of
  what you won or lost or what they won or lost, but in
  terms of what was best in this particular situation.

Principled negotiation is not easy, but it has a much higher chance
of long-term success than negotiation based on confrontation and
point-scoring.

In contract negotiations it can seem that 'they' have all the power
because they have the money. Never lose sight of the fact that
negotiations are two-sided. You have something they want: the
ability to provide a good service, responsive to users and the
community, flexible and good value for money. Hold on to your
strengths.

Preparing for negotiations

One key to successful negotiations is developing an attitude which
sees a negotiation as a problem to be solved jointly by all the
participants. Another key to success lies in careful preparation:

In *Successful Negotiation* (see Chapter 2), Robert Maddux lists seven
key steps in approaching negotiations.

- Define goals and objectives.
- Clarify the issues.
- Gather information.
- Humanise and set the climate.
- Prepare for conflict.
- Prepare for compromise and resolution of the issues.
- Prepare for agreement and confirmation.

In defining goals and objectives, keep in mind the difference
between **needs** and **wants**. What do you **need** from the negotiation,
and what do you **want** from it? What do you have to get to meet
your needs? What are you willing to give up to get what you need?
Concentrate on meeting needs first, then wants. In negotiating a
contract, work through the draft point by point and clarify what is
and is not acceptable, and why.

Think through the issues: what is important for you and why, and how you can best present your views to the other party in a way which helps them to understand what you are saying. Equally importantly, think through what issues are likely to be important for the other party, and how they are likely to respond to the issues which you present. What are likely to be the significant differences between your views and theirs? What are the implications of those differences in terms of services, your users, your organisation? Concentrate first on points of shared concern. Remember, you and they may have differing views but that does not make them stupid, or wrong, or your enemy.

Having found out all you can about the issues, now find out about the people you will be negotiating with, where the negotiations will be held, and how much time will be available.

Humanising and setting the climate means ensuring that you are going into the negotiations wanting to establish a good working relationship, rather than approaching them in a confrontational or adversarial style.

Prepare for conflict by thinking through the likely points of major conflict and considering how you will deal with them. Then, remembering that your concern is not just to get what you need but also to ensure that the other party gets what they need, prepare for compromise and resolution of the issues. Don't be afraid of conflict, but don't hang on to it unnecessarily. Plan to use any conflict as a starting point for clarifying what both parties need and working together to find ways to meet those needs.

Last but not least, be clear beforehand what the processes are for getting approval. Do you, as negotiator, have the right to agree to proposals? Or do the proposals have to go back to the contracts sub-committee or the management committee? This should be clear before anyone enters the negotiation room.

Negotiating a contract

Look again at Chapter 5, at the distinction between a **statement** and an **offer**. Be clear when you are making an offer, and whenever it is mentioned in writing mark it **'subject to contract'**. This should ensure that your organisation only enters a binding agreement when the formal contract is signed.

Before a negotiating session starts, clarify who will keep formal notes or minutes and how these will be circulated to the other party or parties. Even if someone else is taking formal notes, always keep your own notes for your organisation. If more than one person from your organisation is taking part in the negotiations, clarify beforehand who will keep notes.

Negotiators for an organisation should take care not to exceed the authority delegated to them. If you need to clear something with the contracts sub-committee or management committee, say so. Do not agree to change your offer without working through the implications for service delivery, management, and cost. This means that negotiations are likely to take several sessions with preparation and revised documentation being produced for each occasion.

If several documents and/or versions are being produced, put a date (and reference number, if appropriate) in the top corner of the first page of each one, so you don't get confused about which is the most recent. Date all correspondence.

Some organisations want to carry out all negotiations in writing; others want to do everything through informal chats or telephone conversations. Beware of either extreme. In face-to-face negotiations each party can discuss its needs and wants and come to understand the other party's needs and wants. It is much easier to come to agreement through this process of 'give and get' than through writing everything down and waiting for a written reply. But face-to-face negotiations should be identified as negotiations and should not be too informal; if they are it may not be clear what has been formally offered and accepted and what has just been informal chat. Be wary of telephone negotiations; it is very easy to misunderstand or misinterpret what is being said.

Everything agreed in verbal (face-to-face or telephone) negotiations should be written down and, if appropriate, sent to the other party for confirmation.

Written documentation

In these early years of large-scale contracting-out of services it is possible that the public body involved will not have a written contract for you to see at the tender stage or during contract negotiations. The expectation may be that after negotiations have taken place, typically with the service department rather than with legal officers, the agreement will be turned into a legal document (the contract itself) by the local authority's or health authority's legal department.

Beware of a reinterpretation of the agreement at this stage! Experience suggests that the public body's lawyers may seek to interpret any agreement in ways that provide the maximum benefit for their authority. So the written contract may not be quite what you expect.

It is important for the voluntary organisation to have its own commercial solicitors look at the contract and ensure that the intentions of any negotiated agreement are properly reflected in the written documentation. This underlines the importance of keeping detailed notes at the negotiation stage.

Starting without a contract

There may well be pressure on the voluntary organisation to start delivering the service before the final details of the contract are negotiated. Try to resist this; it could severely weaken your arguing position in relation to the final contract. You could also end up in serious financial difficulty if the purchaser decides not to go ahead with the contract.

What happens if your grant runs out on 31 March and you still don't have a contract for the new financial year? You are hardly likely to close your hostel or community nursery on 1 April just because you don't have the right piece of paper on your desk.

Anticipate this situation well in advance; start hassling the local or other authority and its legal department in January or February. If by mid-March you still have nothing, write to the purchaser outlining all the points which have been agreed so far, and say that from 1 April you will operate under these agreed points as a binding contract, until they produce the actual document. Give them a deadine to confirm in writing that this is acceptable. Remember, a contract can exist even without a 'proper' legal document. If two parties have agreed, with the intention of creating a legally binding agreement, that one will provide a service and the other will pay for it, then a contract exists - even if nothing is written down.

If you get to the cut-off date without even having negotiated agreement with the purchaser about what services will be provided and what you will be paid for them, you are in trouble. A management decision will have to be made about how to proceed. Do not treat lightly the potential financial implications of carrying on a service without guaranteed income.

12. Tendering for a contract

The legal requirements

A tender is an invitation to make an offer to provide specified goods or services. Although the situation may be different for other public bodies (and should be investigated), the legal requirements on local authorities regarding the tendering process are relatively weak. The **general requirement** is that they should observe their own standing orders. These are likely to be based on model standing orders issued by the Department of the Environment. Local authorities may extend these. The aim of these standing orders is to ensure that contracts are let in a way which conforms to financial propriety and is in accordance with policy.

Under the Local Government Act 1988 and subsequent parliamentary orders, local authorities must put certain **defined activities** out to competitive tender. This process is referred to as **compulsory competitive tender (CCT)**, and the defined activities are collection of refuse, cleaning of buildings, other cleaning, catering for schools and welfare, other catering, grounds maintenance, repair and maintenance of vehicles, and management of sports and leisure. The Secretary of State for the Environment can, through parliamentary order, add other activities to this list.

In the CCT process, local authorities must comply with some specific requirements. These include:

- Give notice of the intention to tender services through local and trade press advertising. This should invite expressions of interest from potential tenderers.
- Formally invite tenders from at least three of those expressing an interest in tendering.
- Award the contract without reference to factors which could distort or prevent competition, and in particular without reference to 'non-commercial' factors.

Non-commercial factors include terms and conditions of employment by contractors for their workers, the conduct of contractors or workers in industrial disputes, the contractor's financial support for any institution, and similar factors.

It might seem that these arrangements leave local authorities considerable scope in the design and application of a tendering process for CCT. But this scope is constrained by the right of any interested tenderer, or an appropriate trade organisation, to appeal to the Secretary of State or to apply to the High Court for a judicial review of the tendering procedure if they think the local authority is not carrying it out properly.

Many local authorities put work out to tender even if they are not legally obliged to do so. This is non-compulsory or **voluntary competitive tendering.** In this situation the local authority has to comply with its own standing orders, and also with Part II of the Local Government Act 1988 which states that local authorities may not specify non-commercial considerations in contracts.

Voluntary organisations should satisfy themselves that the tendering process being adopted by the local authority or other public body is in accordance with the body's standing orders and fulfils any tendering requirements set out in legislation. The question to be asked is whether the public body is using procedures which enable it to enter into a legally binding relationship. If it does not properly follow the right procedures, the contract could be declared invalid.

Local authorities and other public bodies can issue contracts without putting the work out to tender. This gives the contractor (voluntary organisation) considerable scope for negotiating the terms of the contract.

The tender specification

A tender specification describes the services, activities or goods which the local authority or other body wants to contract for. It is generally in two parts. The **service specification** sets out what is to be done or provided, who the service is for, when it will be provided, quality expectations and similar matters relating directly to the service. The **contract specification** sets out the terms under which the service or goods are to be provided.

For compulsory tendering, and in some cases for non-compulsory tendering, the local authority or other purchaser body will draw up the tender specification. A voluntary organisation might seek to influence the tender specification, especially to ensure that qualitative measures of performance are included. But it is important to be aware of the possibility of allegations of conflict of interest if a voluntary organisation which intends to bid for a contract has undue influence on the tender specification.

Sometimes with non-compulsory tendering the purchaser might place the onus on the tendering organisations to specify what service they will offer on what terms. In this case a voluntary organisation will need to 'second-guess' what the local authority or other body wants to provide and what other tendering organisations will offer.

Service specification

If an existing service is being contracted out the starting point for preparing the tender specification should be the preparation of a **service profile** by the local authority department or other public body. It should include information such as:

- the scope of the service currently provided;
- the level, quantity and frequency of the service;
- details of how the service is provided;
- the number and nature of existing jobs;
- the types of employees;
- training requirements;
- the facilities and equipment used;
- revenue and capital budgets.

But is this the way that the service can or should be operated in the future? A sensible local authority department will undertake some research with staff and users to see whether there are areas of operation which could be improved. The service profile should then be amended to build in proposed improvements.

From the service profile the **service specification** can be developed. This should set out the work to be done, the standards to be achieved, and the methods to be employed to attain these standards. For a new service there will not be a profile of the existing service, so the service specification will be based on research and political decisions about what is needed.

The service specification should set standards for quality of service and staffing. These might include, for example:
- qualifications and skills of workers;
- health and safety;
- nationally agreed service standards;
- types of machinery and materials;
- methods of consultation with users and responsiveness to users.

If the purchaser has not prepared a service profile or issued an adequately detailed service specification, the voluntary organisation may need to create them. This may involve a great deal of research and preparation, especially if information is not easily available about services currently provided and the cost of providing them.

If a voluntary organisation develops its own service specification, it will be worthwhile checking the general terms with the potential purchaser before proceeding. However, beware of being too specific and thereby creating expectations about the quality and extent of the service which you cannot subsequently meet within the purchaser's budget.

Be aware also that your service specification may be a 'hot property' for competitors; it represents a considerable investment of your resources, and a considerable saving of their own resources. So be careful about handing out copies at this stage, even to the potential purchaser. This is where significant issues arise about whether competitive tendering will lead to unseemly competitiveness and lack of cooperation among voluntary organisations, and about whether small or specialist organisations will have the resources to compete with the larger and better-resourced organisations.

Contract specification

The contract specification sets out the terms for the work, including:

- the length of the contract;
- the frequency of payment;
- price review periods;
- lease arrangements in respect of any property and equipment to be made available by the purchaser;
- transitional arrangements in respect of any staff to be transferred from the purchaser's existing workforce;
- monitoring periods and monitoring information required.

Each of these items will have important implications when costing the specification.

Costing and pricing

From the service and contract specifications you can cost the service. It is helpful to do this with some idea of what the purchaser is willing to pay. But you may well not have this information, because the purchaser will be waiting to see who puts in the lowest bid.

If the purchaser has issued a tender with a detailed specification you will have little flexibility about what you provide. The task is to find the most economical way of delivering the service, including the achievement of the quality criteria. You need to be looking for the most efficient way of organising service delivery, and at the cost of the various resources you will need to use: staff, buildings, equipment, raw materials, administration.

Beware of arbitrarily cutting costs if the outcome is higher than you think the purchaser will pay. If you tender at a price below your real cost either you will not be able to deliver the service required, or you will have to subsidise the service from other sources. Chapter 10 looks at costing and pricing issues in more detail.

If you have prepared the service specification yourself, you are likely to have more flexibliity at the costing/pricing stage. If you judge that your price is too high you can either revise the specification (committing yourself to less work or a lower quality of provision) or can try to persuade the purchaser to increase their budget, in order to pay for the service they and the users require.

When pricing work be sure to build in a reasonable figure for contingencies. You should also consider the need to build up reserves to develop the organisation.

Submitting the tender bid

For compulsory competitive tendering, a local authority must advertise its intention to put the service out to tender, and must invite expressions of interest from contractors. It will then invite at least three of the interested parties to submit bids.

For non-compulsory competitive tendering a purchaser may simply advertise for bids or invite bids from contractors on an approved list.

The tender specification may indicate the form in which the bid is to be submitted. If so, follow all instructions carefully.

Make sure your bid is dated and clearly states the organisation's name, address, telephone and fax numbers, and the name and position of the contact person. Present your information clearly and concisely. Don't waffle; don't include unnecessary information; don't use vague words like 'some' or 'frequent'. Number paragraphs or sections for ease of reference. Use a typewriter or word processor with a good ribbon. Keep photocopies of everything.

Deadlines are important and for competitive tendering cannot be stretched. Allow enough time for the necessary consulation, decision-making and preparation. A bid drawn up at midnight the night before it is due may end up with errors or omissions which later prove significant.

If accepted your bid will usually be taken as your final offer. But it may be subject to further negotiation, especially if considerable time has elapsed since the bid was prepared or if circumstances have changed in some way. Beware of changes at this stage without carefully reconsidering the implications for service delivery and cost. A sensible precaution may be to include a date at which the terms of this offer expire, so you have the chance to revise prices to take account of changed circumstances.

13. Assessing quality of service

A voluntary organisation providing services under a contract and the purchaser of those services (local authority, health authority etc) are both committed to quality, and have an interest in defining the expected level of quality. But difficulties can arise if 'quality' is defined too closely; the organisation may not be able to meet changing needs, and a failure to meet the required quality could lead to termination of the contract. On the other hand difficulties can also occur if the required quality is not defined closely enough; disputes may arise about what should or should not have been provided.

Quality may relate to the actual services provided, the processes by which those services are provided, the way the services are managed, or the way the organisation as a whole is managed. Obviously these categories overlap.

It is not enough just to say 'we want to provide a good welfare advice service', 'we want to provide good support for our residents' or 'we want to involve users in all decisions about our services'. Good service, good support and adequate levels of involvement must be defined in some way - otherwise how will you or anyone else know whether you are providing it?

The criteria by which services or management are assessed may be called **measures of quality** or **performance indicators**. Purchasers of services may be primarily concerned to show that the services provide 'value for money' and are 'cost effective'. This may be assessed primarily in financial and quantitative terms: cost per unit of service, perhaps compared with comparable costs of someone else providing a similar service.

In this type of quantitative assessment there is little concern for quality of service. If purchasers of service do look at qualitative factors, they may assess the organisation against criteria with which the organisation disagrees or which are not appropriate to its activities or philosophy.

Providing the best possible service within the constraints of budget and time should be the primary concern of every voluntary organisation. For voluntary organisations entering into contracts it takes on an added importance, because contract renewal may depend on whether agreed quality has been achieved.

It is important for voluntary organisations and their users to set their own measures of quality. To do this, start by asking these questions.

- What services are being provided? This might require a detailed breakdown of exactly what the organisation does and who it does it with or for.

- What needs are the services expected to meet? How were these needs determined?

- How do we know whether we are meeting those needs? Is success determined by quantitative factors (numbers of users, amount of time etc) or by qualitative factors (type of services, intensity of commitment, changes in users' skills or attitudes, solution of a problem or removal of a need)?

- Are special needs being met, which might require a higher input of work to achieve the desired outcomes? (For example, is a housing project seeking to meet the needs of people who simply need housing, or is it seeking to meet the needs of people who need housing *and* need personal or social support?)

- Who defines the desired level of performance or quality for our services? What is the relative input of users, staff, management committee, professionals, and the local authority or health authority which is purchasing the service? Are there nationally or locally agreed criteria which must be used, or which could form a starting point for our own assessment?

- What might the desired level(s) of quality or performance be for each service?

- Should a minimum acceptable level of quality or performance be defined? If so, how?
- Having defined the desirable level of quality or performance, what criteria could used to assess whether this has been achieved?
- Who sets these criteria?
- What information needs to be collected to ensure that achievement of quality or performance can be assessed?
- Who will collect this information?
- Who will evaluate the information?
- How - and how frequently - will the information be presented to the purchaser?
- How are changing needs assessed? How are new performance criteria set?
- Will quality or performance criteria be incorporated into the contract, or set out in an appendix or schedule attached to the contract, or set out in correspondence or a memorandum, or informally agreed?

Monitoring: collecting information

Monitoring is the process of collecting information which can be used in the evaluation of quality or performance.

Statistics

The simplest form of monitoring is quantitative: based on quantities or numbers. It is not difficult to devise record-keeping forms and procedures to collect this sort of information, if the questions above are considered.

But even when these questions have been answered, procedural guidelines are essential. For example, it may seem quite straightforward to collect information about numbers of users. But if a user comes in for a while in the morning, goes away then comes back in the afternoon, is she or he counted once or twice? There are no rules; each organisation must decide for itself - and having decided, must be consistent.

If it is important to monitor the number of different people who use the project *each week*, they should only be counted once in the week. If *daily* use needs to be monitored, users should be counted once for the day. If it is important to monitor the number of people who attend *each session*, they should be counted for each session. Guidelines such as these must be established before monitoring starts or as soon as anyone becomes aware that there is confusion or a discrepancy in the way information is being collected.

Statistical monitoring seeks to be objective. If two people monitor the same work, they should come up with the same results.

Some types of statistical information that might be collected are numbers of sessions, type of services, numbers of users, type of users, attendance rates, occupancy rates, sources of referral to the organisation, outcomes for users.

Analysis of performance

For some types of work it can be appropriate to set standards for the way work is done, or criteria by which performance will be assessed. It is important that these be agreed beforehand, and that the timescales and procedures for assessment are also agreed.

Analysis of outcomes

It may in some situations be appropriate to assess an organisation's effectiveness in terms of outcomes: how many people rehoused, new skills learned by users, greater user involvement in the management committee. Again, it is important to clarify beforehand which outcomes will be assessed, and how. It is also essential to clarify what happens if the outcomes are different from what was expected. It may be impossible to rehouse residents because new accommodation simply is not available; people may not have gained the expected skills but gained instead in confidence or language.

Financial monitoring

While financial costs are not a measure of quality of service, they will inevitably be used as an indicator of the organisation's effectiveness in doing what it was supposed to do within an agreed budget. Good financial management is a measure of quality of management, and this has spin-off effects on quality of service. Good systems for financial record-keeping, reporting and decision-making are essential.

Observation by researcher

Monitoring can be based on observations by the person or people responsible for it. This tends to be subjective (based on a person's interpretation of what is going on) rather than objective (based on information which can be proved in some way). For example, if a trainer says 15 people attended a course and they covered certain topics, that is objective information (assuming it is true); if the trainer says people participated 'a lot' and 'seemed to enjoy themselves' that is subjective.

Subjective observations can be very useful but beware of hidden bias and prejudices which influence how information is interpreted.

Feedback from users or members

Good monitoring directly and systematically involves an organisation's users, participants or members. Ideally this should be done formally, by asking them specific questions on a written questionnaire or in an interview. These questions can be open or closed.

With closed questions the range of possible answers is defined by the questioner. They might be simple yes/no questions or multiple choice. 'Did you feel the service was useful to you?' is a closed question, as is 'Which of the following aspects of the service were most useful to you? Tick one or more.'

Open questions allow people being questioned to frame the answer in their own words. 'How was the service useful to you?' and 'How could the service have been more useful to you?' are open questions.

Open questions usually bring out more information and feelings but it is difficult to analyse the information, because everyone uses different language and talks or writes about things in different ways. Closed questions elicit less information but it is more easily collated.

Good monitoring usually requires a combination of open and closed questions. It should of course involve a wide range of people broadly representative of the organisation's users.

Informal monitoring involves simply chatting to people or eavesdropping on conversations. This is not usually very satisfactory. A statement that 'people said it was great' might be based simply on overhearing one or two people say they really liked whatever it was; it is not necessarily a representative view.

Meetings or special sessions can be held at which users give their views about the organisation and its services. Ensure that the users who attend are a representative selection, and that quiet, shy or inarticulate users are not overwhelmed by the noisier and more outspoken people.

Review

Monitoring on its own achieves nothing; it simply means the collection of information. The next step is review: looking back at a specific project or activity or at a defined time period, and putting the monitoring data in a usable form. A review is a statement of what happened based on the available information, and will form the basis for the subsequent evaluation of the service.

As with monitoring, a review should be as objective and comprehensive as possible. The easiest way to conduct a review is to have done careful monitoring during the project.

Reviews often include people's observations or their interpretations of events. These can differ from person to person, so a representative selection should be included.

Evaluation

An evaluation is an assessment of:

- whether the organisation has met its objectives and if not, why not;
- whether the work was worth doing;
- whether it met the agreed criteria for acceptable quality or performance, and if not, why not;
- whether the quality or performance criteria should be changed;
- whether resources were well used;
- what remains to be done.

Effective evaluation of a service involves four essentials:

- the **objectives** for the service must be clear right from the beginning, and must be written down;
- the **criteria** by which performance will be assessed must be clear;
- there must be adequate **information** about what happened, so monitoring must have taken place throughout the period and the information collected must have been carefully collated and reviewed;
- the people doing the evaluating must be willing to be critical of their organisation, themselves, and their activities. There is no point evaluating something if people will not be able to bear admitting they did not really achieve what they set out to do. But this **critical approach** can be at odds with a contractual obligation to 'prove' that agreed objectives have indeed been fully met.

Evaluation can only be really useful if there is also a fifth factor:

- after the evaluation people must be willing to **change** or allow the organisation to change. Again, this can be difficult if a contract defines performance too closely.

Presenting evaluation data

An evaluation report should include:

- what the organisation wanted to achieve through providing this service (its objectives);
- background information about the organisation and why these objectives were prioritised;
- the criteria by which achievement of the objectives was assessed;
- what information was collected, and how it was collected and analysed;
- what the information shows;
- whether the original objectives were met;
- what else was achieved;
- new needs which have become apparent, and what the organisation proposes to do about them.

It is dishonest to lie, but it is not dishonest to present information in the most positive way. Stress the good points: what the organisation achieved, what needs it met, the variety of users or activities. If objectives or performance targets were not reached indicate why, and mention what steps are being taken to try to set more realistic objectives. If unanticipated factors prevented the organisation from doing all it wanted to, mention them briefly.

The process of setting performance objectives, monitoring and evaluation should not be seen as repressive procedures imposed by hyper-critical purchasers of services. They are tools for good management and for ensuring voluntary organisations serve their communities and users or members in the best possible way.

14. Getting ready for contracts: a checklist

Getting ready for the contract culture requires, first and foremost, a clear understanding of the organisation's objectives and priorities, and its strengths and limitations. Next it requires time: to discuss what the changes will mean, to ensure adequate consultation and discussion, to set up any necessary systems.

This checklist outlines some of the issues which voluntary organisations should consider before moving into the contract culture, and especially before taking on new activities. The list is not exhaustive; each organisation's checklist will be different.

In general

Regardless of type or size of contract, four broad areas of concern emerge: legal and constitutional issues, issues for service delivery and users, staffing and staff management issues, and finance and funding issues.

Before dealing with those issues, there are two essential questions:

- How will we find the necessary time to ensure that staff and management committee have the information they need and to ensure that decisions are made in a proper way?

- What additional funds will we need to prepare for and take on contracts? Extra costs might include training, legal advice, specialist financial advice, advice on service delivery issues, and typing assistance.

Legal and constitutional issues

- Does the proposed activity or service fall within the organisation's constitutional objectives?
- Are there any constitutional limits on the organisation's beneficiaries or area of benefit? Will the proposed activity fit within those limits?
- Does the organisation have the constitutional power to take on the activity?
- If the organisation is a charity, will the activity fall completely within the charity's primary purpose(s)?
- Is there a need to consider setting up a separate trading company to take on the contract?
- If the organisation will be tendering for a contract, do the people involved understand the tender specification? Do they have the knowledge and skills to draw up a bid?
- Is the existing management structure appropriate for managing the activity? Or will it need some sort of new or separate management body? If there are two management bodies, is any cross-accountability required?
- If the organisation has a two-tier management structure (for example charity trustees and a separate management committee) what part does each body play in the decision whether to take on a contract?
- If the organisation is a limited company or an industrial and provident society, *and* it is not a registered charity, *and* it has people associated with the local authority on its management body, is it affected by the provisions of the Local Government Act 1989 on local authority controlled and influenced companies?
- Does the contract involve a conflict of interest for any member of the management body? If so, how does this affect their part in the decision-making process?
- If users form part (or all) of the current management body, will this continue with any new management body? If users are not now on the management body, should they be?
- Are members of the management body aware of their

legal responsibilities for the contract? What steps need to be taken to limit their liability, and to ensure they have the necessary knowledge and information to undertake their responsibilities?

- If a limited company is to be set up, will the organisation be able to cope with the required paperwork?

- Do the members of the management body (and others involved in the consultative and decision-making processes) have the skills and knowledge to understand the issues involved in the decision whether to take on the contract? If not, how can they be helped towards this understanding?

- Do members of the management body have the skills and knowledge to manage the activity and the contract? If not, how can the management body be strengthened? What are the spin-off effects (positive and negative) of increased professionalisation of the management body?

- Is some sort of liaison body needed to ensure proper communication between the purchaser (local authority etc) and the contractor (voluntary organisation)? How will the users' views be taken into account?

- Is the organisation aware of sources of specialist legal and financial advice? Can it build up relevant contacts?

- If legal and financial expertise has to be brought in, who will pay for it? Is there a conflict of interest in the purchaser (local authority etc) paying for legal advice for the contractor (voluntary organisation)?

- Does the organisation keep up-to-date with new publications about contracts and other relevant changes in the voluntary sector?

- Is the organisation discussing these issues with other relevant local, regional and national organisations, in order to draw on their experience?

Service delivery and users

- What new opportunities can the proposed activity provide?

- Does the organisation have a clear 'mission' or purpose?

Does it have clear objectives and priorities? Do people know what they are? Does the proposed activity fit in with them?

- Does the organisation have a clear ethos, philosophy or approach, and is it known and shared by users, staff, and members of the management body? Does the proposed activity fit with this philosophy?
- How will existing activities be affected by any new activity?
- Is there a risk of the organisation moving in new many directions at once, or taking on too many new activities?
- Will the new activity meet the needs of people from all relevant ethnic or cultural groups? Will it be suitable for people with special needs?
- If a new activity represents a significant change in direction and/or philosophy, how (if at all) will users be involved in the decision whether to take it on?
- How will users be influenced by any changes created by a new activity? Will users need help or support to cope with these changes?
- How and by whom will quality of service be assessed? What say will users have in this?
- Are there ways to 'top up' this service to make it better or to enable it to meet special or additional needs, perhaps through fundraising or the use of volunteers?
- Does the contract involve significant changes in the scale of the organisation's activity and in the way the organisation is managed or administered? If so, will users need help or support to understand these changes?
- What training or support is required to ensure that staff can provide new or expanded services?
- What training or support is required to enable staff to work with new users?
- Will the new activity enable the organisation to acquire new equipment or replace existing equipment?
- What is the likely impact of not taking on the activity? How will it affect users?

- What would be the effect on the organisation's credibility, or its relationship with the local or other statutory authority of it did not take on the activity?
- What are the threats (e.g redundancies, closure) if a new activity or contract is not taken on?

Staffing and staff management

- To what extent should staff be involved in any decision? How will they be informed, consulted or involved in the decision?
- What are the possible effects of rapid staff expansion?
- What training or support will staff need?
- Will the proposed activity involve greater use of volunteers? How will they be recruited, trained and supported? How will the organisation ensure that volunteers are not treated as 'cheap labour'?
- Will the proposed activity involve decreased use of volunteers? How will this affect the organisation's philosophy and general approach?
- If new activities are to be taken on, or if existing activities are to be substantially expanded, what are the implications of having a centralised or a devolved structure for day-to-day management?
- Will the new activities involve a management style which is different from the current approach?
- If the new activity is on a different site or sites, what are the implications of managing staff on several sites?
- How can staff morale be maintained during a period of change?

Finance and funding

- What levels of financial security does a contract offer?
- What financial information is required to submit a bid for a service which has been put out for tender?
- What financial information is required to submit a budget as the basis for negotiating a contract?

- Does the organisation have the necessary expertise to draw up budgets and cashflows, monitor income and expenditure, and make financial decisions? What support is required to ensure the finance workers, staff managers, treasurer and management committee have the necessary expertise?
- If the organisation is not already registered for VAT, will it have register?
- Will the proposed activity be fully self-financing (including its share of premises, admin and other indirect costs/overheads), or will it have to be subsidised by other parts of the organisation or from outside funding sources?
- Will the proposed activity generate enough income that it can subsidise other, under-funded parts of the organisation?
- Does the organisation have enough reserves to cover its cashflow?
- Does the organisation have access to an overdraft or loan facilities?
- Has adequate provision been made for maintaining, replacing or upgrading vehicles and equipment?
- Has adequate provision been made for maintaining and repairing premises and the facilities which will be used?
- Who owns equipment, vehicles and premises? What happens to assets at the end of the contract?
- If payment is to be on a cost per unit basis, what happens if the organisation underperforms, i.e. if it does not work with enough 'units' to generate the anticipated income?
- If payment is to be on a fixed fee basis, what happens if the organisation overperforms, i.e. if it ends up doing more work than anticipated and therefore needs additional income?
- What happens if a surplus is generated (for whatever reason)? Can the organisation keep it, or are there provisions for the local authority or other purchaser to 'claw back' some or all of the surplus?

- If the organisation decides not to take on a contract, or does not get a contract for which it has bid, does this jeopardise its future? What funding alternatives are there?

- What arrangements will there be for reviewing and renewing the contract?

- What happens if the contract is not renewed? How much notice will there be so that alternative sources of funding can be sought, new methods of working or providing services can be implemented or, in the worst case, the organisation can be wound up in a planned way?

- If the organisation is running several different activities under different contracts, what happens if one contract is not renewed? Does this affect the costing or viability of the others?

Taking over existing services

Increasingly the voluntary sector, as well as the commercial sector, will be expected to take over services currently provided by local authorities and other statutory bodies. For a voluntary organisation considering such a step, all of the questions listed above need to be asked, as well as many more.

Legal and constitutional issues

- Have the organisation's management body and staff discussed the political implications of taking on services previously provided by the local authority, health authority or education authority?

- What say will the statutory authority want in managing the activity? Will they want a place on the management committee, and if so will they have a vote?

- How secure is the contract politically?

- What are the legal issues around continuity of employment? (see Staffing, below)

- Who will own any premises? Who will be responsible for maintaining them? Who will be responsible for insuring them?

Service delivery and users

- Will the organisation continue to provide the same type of activity or service as the statutory authority has been providing, or will there be changes?
- Does the statutory authority's service fit in with the voluntary organisation's services?
- How will differences in philosophy or approach be reconciled? Do they need to be reconciled, or can they co-exist?
- How will different user groups, or groups with differing needs, be incorporated into the organisation?
- Who will refer potential users? Who has the final say?
- How will existing users of the statutory service and the voluntary organisation's services be affected by the changes?
- Will expansion mean increased bureaucratisation and professionalisation? How will this affect users?

Staffing and staff management

- How can staff be involved at an early stage, in order to minimise rumours and antagonism?
- Will staff from the statutory service have continuity of employment in their new employment? What are the financial implications of this?
- How will staff job descriptions need to be changed?
- How will staff conditions of employment need to be changed?
- What will be done about wage differentials between workers in the statutory service and the voluntary organisation?
- If staff are to be made redundant, how will this be negotiated?
- How will staff management structures need to be changed?
- How will such changes be negotiated?

- What is the role of the unions, especially if the services being merged or taken over have different traditions of union involvement?
- What will be the role of volunteers?
- Will additional management skills and/or time be needed?
- Will additional admin skills and/or time be needed?
- Are staff supervision arrangements satisfactory?
- Are staff training arrangments satisfactory?
- What arrangements will be made for cover during holidays, etc?

Finance and funding

- How can the voluntary organisation find out what the statutory service has actually cost? Especially the hidden costs which have been absorbed by other statutory authority departments (such as personnel, finance, building maintenance and repairs, vehicle maintenance and repairs).
- Is the statutory authority trying to get the service on the cheap by contracting it out to a voluntary organisation?
- What are the financial implications of different pay scales, increments, sickness and holiday cover, redundancy arrangements, etc?
- Who will own the assets now owned and used by the local authority?

The other way around

These questions have focused primarily on the implications of taking on the contract. Last but not least, ask one more question:

- What happens to our services, our users, our jobs and our organisation if we don't take on the contract?

If your organisation has thought seriously about these issues and has discovered its own answers to these and related questions, you are ready for contracts.

TWELVE CHARITY CONTRACTS

CASE STUDIES OF FUNDING CONTRACTS BETWEEN CHARITIES AND LOCAL AUTHORITIES AND OTHER FUNDING BODIES

The emerging 'Contract Culture' will affect the majority of service providing charities. Contractual relationships with funders will require new approaches and new skills. Read here about the experiences of those who have already entered this field, and see the text of the contracts they have signed.

Charities featured include:

Nuneaton Asian Women's Assn.
Age Concern Cornwall
Groundwork Oldham/Rochdale
Birmingham Council for Old People
Cartrefi Cymru
Kent Volunteer Bureaux
North West Fellowship
Newport MIND

Case studies of funding contracts between charities and local authorities and other bodies

by ANNE DAVIES & KEN EDWARDS

The Contract Culture Series

About the publisher

The Directory of Social Change is an educational charity established in 1975. It is based in London and has a Northern Office in Merseyside. It aims to promote the effective use of charitable resources. It does this by:

Publishing a range of grant guides, advisory handbooks and information sources on all aspects of fundraising and charity management.

Organising a national programme of training courses in fundraising, financial management, communication skills, management skills and personal skills. These courses are aimed exclusively at charities and voluntary organisations.

Organising conferences and seminars on matters of current interest.

Undertaking and publishing research.

Developing pilot initiatives.

Further information from the **Directory of Social Change**, Radius Works, Back Lane, London NW3 1HL (071-435 8171).